# Mac OS® X Tiger™
## Top 100

# Simplified®

## TIPS & TRICKS

by Mark Chambers

Visual

WILEY

# Mac OS® X Tiger™ Top 100 Simplified® Tips & Tricks

Published by
Wiley Publishing, Inc.
111 River Street
Hoboken, NJ 07030-5774

Published simultaneously in Canada

Copyright © 2005 by Wiley Publishing, Inc., Indianapolis, Indiana

Library of Congress Control Number: 2005923190

ISBN-13: 978-0-7645-7699-7

ISBN-10: 0-7645-7699-2

Manufactured in the United States of America

10 9 8 7 6 5 4 3 2 1

1K/QW/QW/QV/IN

## Trademark Acknowledgments

## Contact Us

For general information on our other products and services contact our Customer Care Department within the U.S. at 800-762-2974, outside the U.S. at 317-572-3993 or fax 317-572-4002.

For technical support please visit www.wiley.com/techsupport.

**WILEY**

Wiley Publishing, Inc.

**Sales**

Contact Wiley at (800) 762-2974 or fax (317) 572-4002.

# PRAISE FOR VISUAL BOOKS

"I have to praise you and your company on the fine products you turn out. I have twelve Visual books in my house. They were instrumental in helping me pass a difficult computer course. Thank you for creating books that are easy to follow. Keep turning out those quality books."
*Gordon Justin (Brielle, NJ)*

"What fantastic teaching books you have produced! Congratulations to you and your staff. You deserve the Nobel prize in Education. Thanks for helping me understand computers."
*Bruno Tonon (Melbourne, Australia)*

"A Picture Is Worth A Thousand Words! If your learning method is by observing or hands-on training, this is the book for you!"
*Lorri Pegan-Durastante (Wickliffe, OH)*

"Over time, I have bought a number of your 'Read Less - Learn More' books. For me, they are THE way to learn anything easily. I learn easiest using your method of teaching."
*José A. Mazón (Cuba, NY)*

"You've got a fan for life!! Thanks so much!!"
*Kevin P. Quinn (Oakland, CA)*

"I have several books from the Visual series and have always found them to be valuable resources."
*Stephen P. Miller (Ballston Spa, NY)*

"I have several of your Visual books and they are the best I have ever used."
*Stanley Clark (Crawfordville, FL)*

"Like a lot of other people, I understand things best when I see them visually. Your books really make learning easy and life more fun."
*John T. Frey (Cadillac, MI)*

"I have quite a few of your Visual books and have been very pleased with all of them. I love the way the lessons are presented!"
*Mary Jane Newman (Yorba Linda, CA)*

"Thank you, thank you, thank you...for making it so easy for me to break into this high-tech world."
*Gay O'Donnell (Calgary, Alberta, Canada)*

"I write to extend my thanks and appreciation for your books. They are clear, easy to follow, and straight to the point. Keep up the good work! I bought several of your books and they are just right! No regrets! I will always buy your books because they are the best."
*Seward Kollie (Dakar, Senegal)*

"I would like to take this time to thank you and your company for producing great and easy-to-learn products. I bought two of your books from a local bookstore, and it was the best investment I've ever made! Thank you for thinking of us ordinary people."
*Jeff Eastman (West Des Moines, IA)*

"Compliments to the chef!! Your books are extraordinary! Or, simply put, extra-ordinary, meaning way above the rest! THANKYOU THANKYOU THANKYOU! I buy them for friends, family, and colleagues."
*Christine J. Manfrin (Castle Rock, CO)*

# CREDITS

**Project Editor**
Jade L. Williams

**Acquisitions Editor**
Jody Lefevere

**Product Development Manager**
Lindsay Sandman

**Copy Editor**
Scott Tullis

**Technical Editor**
Maarten Reilingh

**Editorial Manager**
Robyn Siesky

**Permissions Editor**
Laura Moss

**Editorial Assistant**
Adrienne Porter

**Manufacturing**
Allan Conley
Linda Cook
Paul Gilchrist
Jennifer Guynn

**Special Help**
Apple Computer, Inc.

**Cover Design**
Anthony Bunyan

**Book Design**
Kathie S. Rickard

**Production Coordinator**
Maridee Ennis

**Layout**
Jennifer Heleine
Amanda Spagnuolo

**Screen Artist**
Elizabeth Cardenas-Nelson
Jill A. Proll

**Illustrators**
Ronda David-Burroughs

**Proofreader**
Melissa D. Buddendeck

**Indexer**
Johnna VanHoose

**Quality Control**
Susan Moritz
Brian H. Walls

**Vice President and Executive
Group Publisher**
Richard Swadley

**Vice President and Publisher**
Barry Pruett

**Composition Director**
Debbie Stailey

# ABOUT THE AUTHOR

Mark L. Chambers (Columbia, Missouri) has been an author, computer consultant, BBS sysop, programmer, and hardware technician for more than 20 years. Mark has written over 15 computer books. Mark is currently a full-time author and tech editor. He has recently branched out into Web-based education, designing and teaching a number of online classes, called WebClinics, for Hewlett Packard. Mark holds degrees in journalism and creative writing from Louisiana State University.

# HOW TO USE THIS BOOK

Mac OS® X Tiger™ Top 100 Simplified® Tips & Tricks includes 100 tasks that reveal cool secrets, teach timesaving tricks, and explain great tips guaranteed to make you more productive. The easy-to-use layout lets you work through all the tasks from beginning to end or jump in at random.

## Who Is This Book For?

You already know Tiger basics. Now you'd like to go beyond, with shortcuts, tricks and tips that let you work smarter and faster. And because you learn more easily when someone *shows* you how, this is the book for you.

## Conventions Used In This Book

### ❶ Steps

This book uses step-by-step instructions to guide you easily through each task. Numbered callouts on every screen shot show you exactly how to perform each task, step by step.

### ❷ Tips

Practical tips provide insights to save you time and trouble, caution you about hazards to avoid, and reveal how to do things in Tiger that you never thought possible!

### ❸ Task Numbers

Task numbers from 1 to 100 indicate which lesson you are working on.

### ❹ Difficulty Levels

For quick reference, symbols mark the difficulty level of each task.

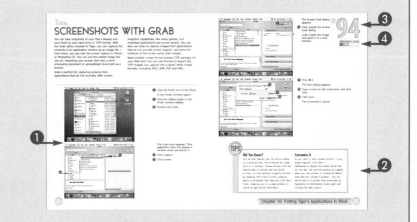

| DIFFICULTY LEVEL | Demonstrates a new spin on a common task |
| DIFFICULTY LEVEL | Introduces a new skill or a new task |
| DIFFICULTY LEVEL | Combines multiple skills requiring in-depth knowledge |
| DIFFICULTY LEVEL | Requires extensive skill and may involve other technologies |

# Table of Contents

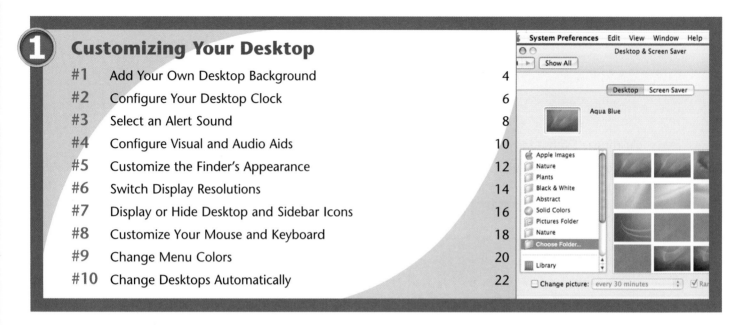

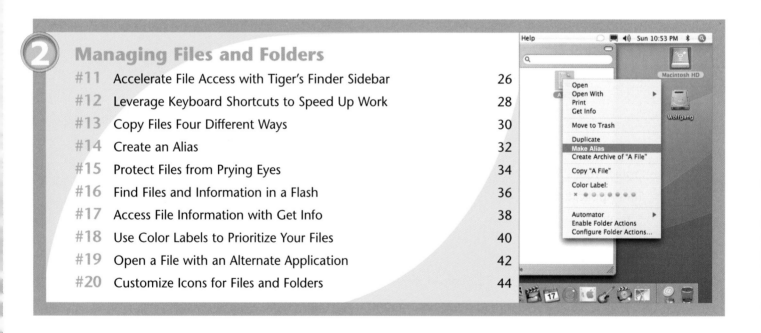

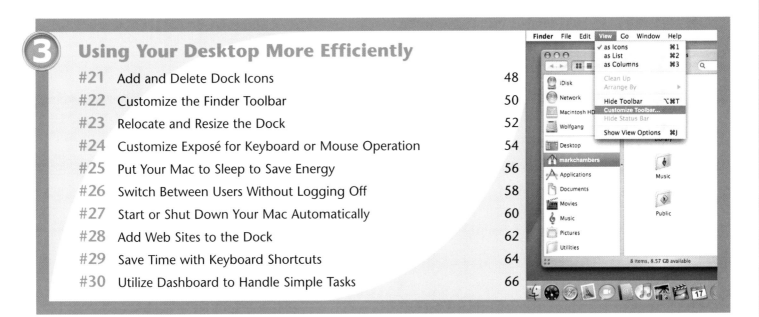

# Using Your Desktop More Efficiently

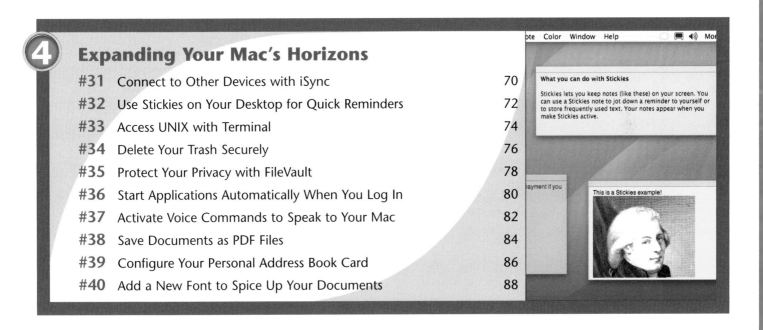

# Expanding Your Mac's Horizons

# Table of Contents

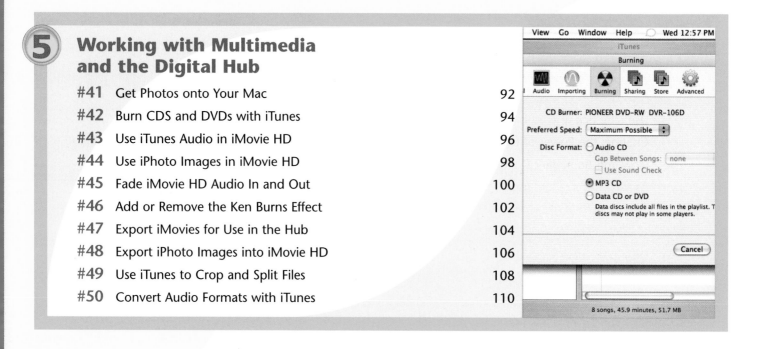

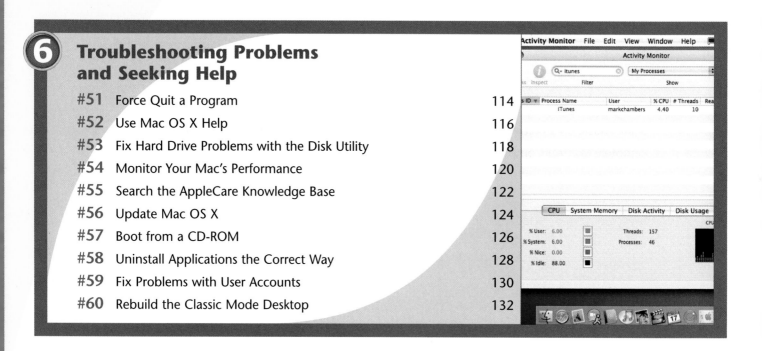

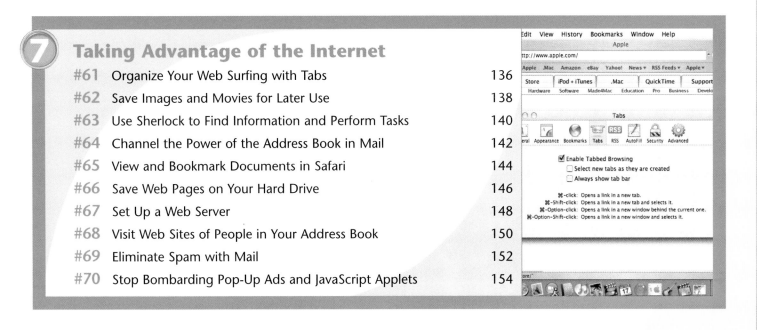

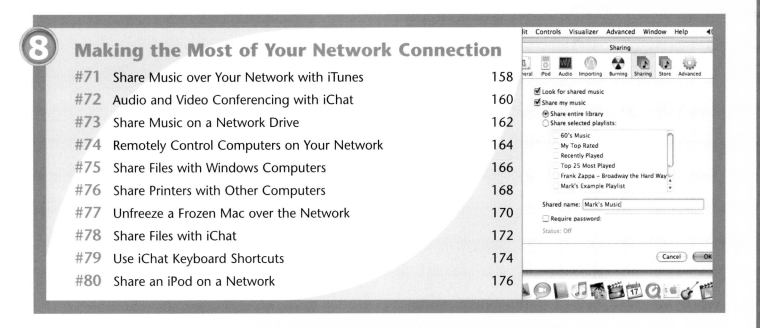

# Table of Contents

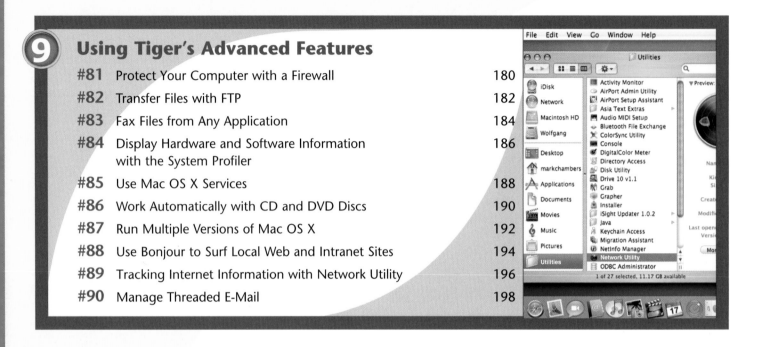
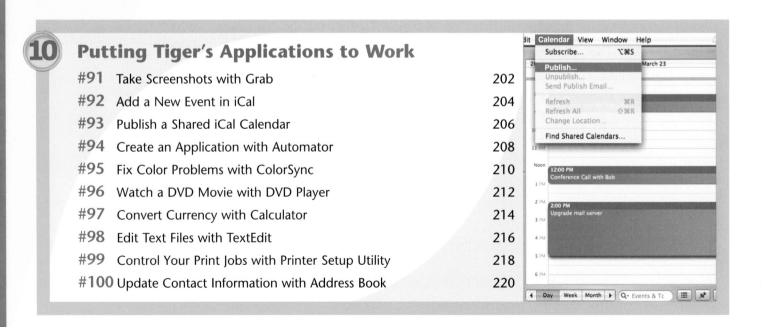

# Customizing Your Desktop

Any Tiger power user knows that customizing the Mac OS X desktop is an important key to improved productivity. After all, if you know where your tools are and have arranged things to your satisfaction, you work faster and with less effort! Even a so-called minor change to the desktop, such as a new background picture, can help a user maintain focus (and keep smiling) after a long day of work.

In fact, many readers think that you have to be a software developer, Hollywood video editor, or a professional musician to warrant customizing the Tiger desktop; this is *definitely* not true. Even if you use your Mac only an hour or so every day, you will enjoy your time

behind the keyboard far more if your desktop is arranged to your preferences. Consider the effect of changing just your video resolution: With only two or three mouse clicks, you immediately have more area available to create and edit your documents.

Most of the tips in this chapter cover changes to the look of your desktop, which makes sense: Because the Macintosh has used a graphical operating system from the very beginning, Mac OS X is a feast for the eyes. You learn the steps to configuring your desktop clock and the Finder window toolbar, as well as features for those with reduced vision.

# Top 100

# Add your own
# DESKTOP BACKGROUND

You can choose your own image as a desktop background for Tiger. Apple ships a number of attractive background images with Mac OS X, including abstract artwork and nature photos, but most computer owners prefer using their own favorite images for a desktop background. In fact, if you have created a library of digital photographs using iPhoto, Tiger makes selecting an image from your library for use as a desktop background easier. You will also find hundreds of sites on the Web that offer a wide selection of desktop images, covering just about every subject imaginable.

Alternatively, you can opt for a solid color background instead of an image; if you are running a laptop or an older Mac desktop, you may find that Tiger performs a little faster when you use a solid color background.

Within Mac OS X, you can use the Desktop & Screen Saver pane in System Preferences to choose an image for your desktop background.

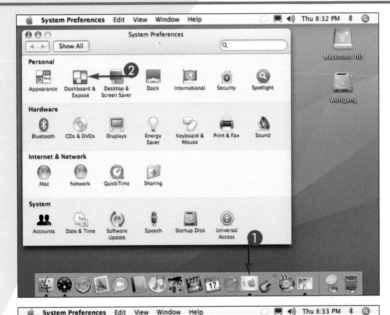

❶ Click the System Preferences icon in the Dock.

The System Preferences window appears.

❷ Click the Desktop & Screen Saver icon.

The Desktop & Screen Saver pane appears.

❸ Click the Desktop tab to select a picture.

❹ Click Choose Folder.

A File Open dialog opens.

⑤ Click the source that holds the image you want to use.

⑥ Double-click the folder that holds the image you want.

If the image is stored in a subfolder, double-click the subfolder to open the subfolder.

⑦ Click Choose to display the pictures in the selected folder.

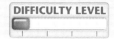

**DIFFICULTY LEVEL**

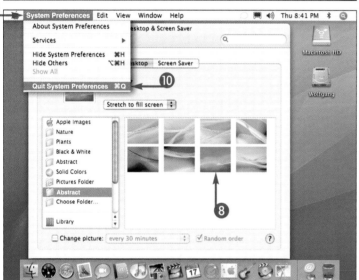

⑧ Click the picture that you want to use.

The selected image appears in the preview well at the top of the dialog.

⑨ Click System Preferences.

⑩ Click Quit System Preferences.

Mac OS X saves your changes and displays your new desktop background.

**TIPS**

### Did You Know?

Although any JPEG or TIFF format image can be used as a background picture, images smaller than 640 x 480 may not look their best covering your full desktop. To use a smaller desktop image, click the Layout drop-down list box on the Desktop & Screen Saver pane and click Tile. Your desktop covers with multiple copies of the image.

### Did You Know?

If you want to use an image that you have stored in your Pictures folder, click Pictures Folder in the Desktop & Screen Saver pane. Tiger immediately displays thumbnails of any images that you have saved to the folder. Because many applications use your Pictures folder as a default location for saving image files, this shortcut can save you time.

**Chapter 1: Customizing Your Desktop** ⑤

# Configure your
# DESKTOP CLOCK

You can easily customize the appearance, behavior, and location of your Mac's desktop clock by using the settings within the Date & Time pane of System Preferences. Apple recognizes the value of a good timepiece, and this is reflected in Mac OS X. If your Mac has a connection to the Internet, you can even use an Internet time server to automatically update your computer's clock at regular intervals.

Tiger provides a great time announcement feature. Click the Announce the Time check box and specify the time period that you want. This automated announcement can help you keep track of passing time while you work.

If you travel with your Mac laptop, you probably need to change the time zone often. Tiger makes this easy. Just select the closest city to your current location in the Time Zone pane, which is also a part of the Date & Time pane. Tiger automatically updates the system time to match your new time zone.

① Click the System Preferences icon in the Dock.

The System Preferences window appears.

② Click the Date & Time icon.

The Date & Time pane appears.

③ Click the Clock tab.

④ Click the Show the date and time check box to enable (☐ changes to ☑).

⑤ Click an option to specify where you want the clock to appear (◯ changes to ◉).

*Note: If you click Window, you can click and drag the clock window to any spot on your desktop.*

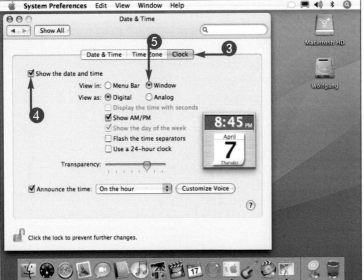

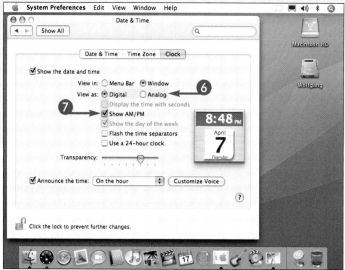

**DIFFICULTY LEVEL**

6 Click an option to select a digital or analog view of the clock (○ changes to ◉).

7 Click options to customize the digital clock display (□ changes to ☑).

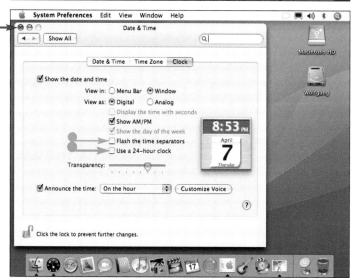

The clock immediately updates to show your changes.

● If you use a digital clock, you can click Flash the time separators to indicate the seconds (□ changes to ☑).

● If you use a digital clock, you can click Use a 24-hour clock to display the time in the 24-hour military fashion (□ changes to ☑).

8 Click the Close button to save your changes and close the System Preferences window.

### Did You Know?

If your Mac has an Internet connection, you can configure Tiger's clock to automatically update the time from an Internet time server. To do so, in the Date & Time pane, click the Set Date & Time Automatically check box to enable the feature. You can then click the check box's drop-down list to select an Apple Internet time server.

### Did You Know?

Tiger enables you to switch to an international format for your clock's date and time. However, all international formats are handled from the International pane in System Preferences; therefore, you will find a convenient Open International button within the Date & Time panel. Click the Open International button to switch to the International pane where you can choose the desired format.

# Select an
# ALERT SOUND

Through the settings on the Sound pane in System Preferences, the Mac OS X desktop can keep you abreast of important events — even if you are across the room — by providing you with an alert sound; or you can decide to eliminate alert sounds entirely for quiet computing. Apple provides a wide variety of alert sounds, so you are sure to find one you prefer.

By default, Tiger plays alert sounds at many points: if an application displays a message or warning dialog, for example, or when you click certain

controls within an application window or system window. You can turn these sounds off, adjust the overall system volume, or mute all sound entirely.

You can control the volume levels of all sound played by your Macintosh, including the audio produced by games and other applications, by using the Sound pane in System Preferences. Adjusting the Output Volume setting is equivalent to pressing the Volume Up or Volume Down keys on your keyboard.

① Click the System Preferences icon in the Dock.

The System Preferences window appears.

② Click the Sound icon.

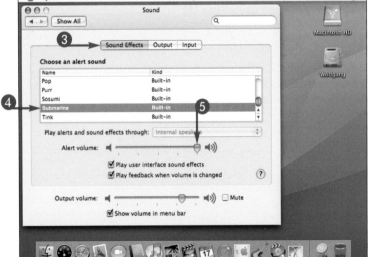

The Sound window appears.

③ Click the Sound Effects tab.

④ Click an alert sound effect.

Tiger plays the sound effect so that you can decide if you like it.

⑤ Drag the Alert volume slider to adjust the sound.

*Note: The volume level is dependent on the overall Output volume. If you raise or lower the Output volume, the Alert volume also changes.*

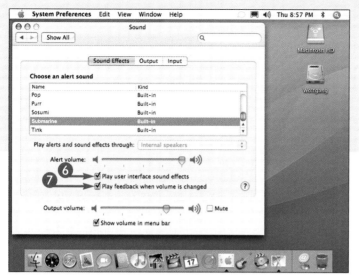

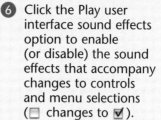

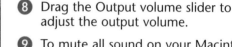

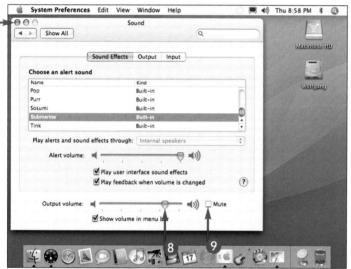

6 Click the Play user interface sound effects option to enable (or disable) the sound effects that accompany changes to controls and menu selections (☐ changes to ☑).

7 Click the Play feedback when volume is changed option to enable (or disable) the sound effects played when you press the Volume Up and Volume Down keys on your keyboard (☐ changes to ☑).

8 Drag the Output volume slider to adjust the output volume.

9 To mute all sound on your Macintosh, click the Mute check box (☐ changes to ☑).

10 Click the Close button to save your changes and close the System Preferences window.

Your new alert sound settings are saved.

**TIPS**

### Did You Know?
Clicking the Mute check box in the Sound pane is handy when you want to turn off all sound on your computer — for example, on your Mac laptop when you are on the road, or for a study period in the library. Using this check box is equivalent to pressing the Mute key on your keyboard.

### Customize It!
If your keyboard does not have volume keys, or if you often need to rapidly change the volume on your system, use your mouse! You can click and drag to adjust the Volume control, located at the far right of the Finder menu, and the Volume icon itself changes to indicate the relative volume setting.

# Configure
# VISUAL AND AUDIO AIDS

You can configure your Mac so that your desktop and applications are easier to see. Today's larger monitors make it easy to configure Mac OS X to cut down on eyestrain and help prevent headaches after several hours at the keyboard. You can set your display to grayscale instead of color — or even to white-on-black — and enhance the contrast of your display to help windows and dialogs stand out. For those who cannot hear the system alert sounds, you can also set Tiger to flash the screen instead.

In Tiger, you can configure visual and audio aids in the Universal Access pane of the System Preferences window. Do not be surprised if you suddenly hear your Macintosh speaking to you while making changes to the settings in the Universal Access pane! If you click the VoiceOver On radio button, Tiger automatically speaks the name of each control on the pane when you move your mouse pointer over it.

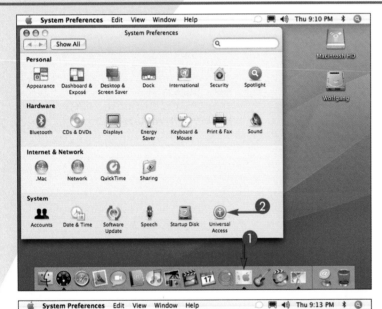

❶ Click the System Preferences icon in the Dock.

The System Preferences window appears.

❷ Click the Universal Access icon.

The Universal Access window appears.

❸ Click the Seeing tab.

❹ Click Zoom On to enable the Zoom feature.

You can select a portion of the screen to zoom by moving the mouse, which moves the preview rectangle.

❺ Press ⌘–Option–= to zoom in on the portion of the screen visible in the window.

❻ Press ⌘–Option–– (the minus sign) to incrementally zoom out again.

❼ Click White on Black to reverse the desktop colors.

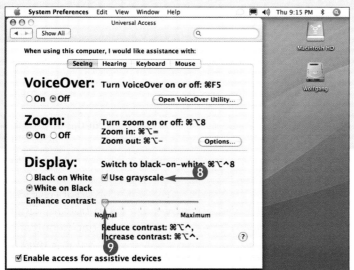

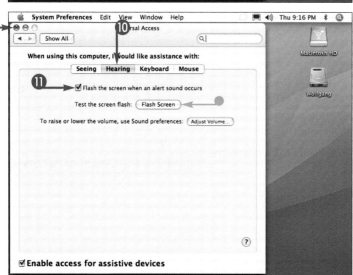

Tiger creates a negative desktop that some Mac users find easier on the eyes.

You can switch between Black on White and White on Black by using the ⌘–Option–Control–8 key sequence.

⑧ Click the Use grayscale option to remove colors.

*Note: This produces a display much like a grayscale photograph, which may help some Mac users who cannot easily distinguish colors.*

⑨ Drag the Enhance contrast slider to increase the contrast.

⑩ Click the Hearing tab.

⑪ Click the Flash the screen when an alert sound occurs to enable the check box (□ changes to ☑).

● To preview the flash effect, you can click Flash Screen.

⑫ Click the Close button to save your changes and close the System Preferences window.

## Did You Know?

You do not have to open the Universal Access pane to toggle the zoom feature on; just press ⌘–Option–8 to turn zoom on, which displays the zoom rectangle. To turn zoom off, press ⌘–Option–8. To toggle the display of the rectangle when you are zoomed out, or to enable image smoothing, click the zoom Options button.

## Did You Know?

If the Zoom window does not appear when you turn on the Zoom feature in the Universal Access pane, you may need to configure the Maximum Zoom setting. Click the Zoom Options button and drag the Maximum Zoom control to a number higher than the default of 1. To zoom past the maximum or minimum settings, hold down ⌘–Option–= (the equal sign) or ⌘–Option–– (the minus sign).

# Customize the
# FINDER'S APPEARANCE

You can customize the appearance of a Finder window to your personal preference. For example, some Mac users prefer the original Icon view, in which files and folders are represented as individual icons, whereas others prefer the List and Column views, in which files and folders are presented in list format. You can perform the same tasks using any of the three view modes, but many Mac users find the Column view faster and more efficient.

Notice the Finder Sidebar — the column on the left of the Finder window that holds items, such as files and folders, and devices, such as hard drives, removable USB drives, and CDs or DVDs. Click an item to open it; if the item is a document, Tiger automatically runs the corresponding application for you. There is more to the Sidebar; it also allows you convenient access to a number of different locations, such as network servers, your Home folder, and your Applications folder.

### SWITCH VIEWS

**①** Press ⌘-N.

Mac OS X displays a new Finder window.

**②** Click the toolbar button to show (or hide) the Finder toolbar.

**③** Click the corresponding View button in the Finder toolbar to toggle between Icon, List, and Column view modes.

*Note: Changing the view mode affects only the current location in your system, for example, the current folder or hard drive.*

**ADD OR REMOVE TOOLBAR BUTTONS**

④ Click View.

⑤ Click Customize Toolbar.

⑥ Drag buttons to and from the toolbar to customize it.

You can drag the default toolbar button set as a whole to reset your toolbar configuration.

⑦ Click Done.

Your changes to the toolbar are saved.

**TIPS**

### Did You Know?

You can click and drag the divider bar to resize the sidebar on the left of the Finder window. Resizing the sidebar may be necessary if you have added a number of folders with longer names; you can also resize the sidebar smaller to make more room for icons or details in the main portion of the Finder window.

### Customize It!

To make changes to all windows displayed with a specific view mode — like the size of the icons in Icon view, or a default sorting order in List view — choose the view mode that you want to configure and press ⌘–J. Make sure that you click All Windows to apply your changes to any window displayed in that mode.

# Switch display
# RESOLUTIONS

You can switch between display resolutions at any time to accommodate different applications and desktop configurations. Mac OS X can use a number of different display resolutions, depending on the combination of graphics cards and monitors that you are using. Some LCD monitors can only use one or two preset display resolutions, while CRT monitors can usually offer a far wider range of display resolutions.

You may want to switch to a higher display resolution when you need to work on a large-format

document — such as a super-sized digital photograph or a detailed PowerPoint slide. A higher display resolution allows you to size windows larger; in games, a higher resolution allows more detail and a more realistic appearance.

There are benefits to using a lower display resolution, however: many Mac users prefer a lower resolution for general readability. Also, laptops and older Macs may deliver faster graphics performance at a lower display resolution.

① Click the System Preferences icon in the Dock.

The System Preferences window appears.

② Click the Displays icon.

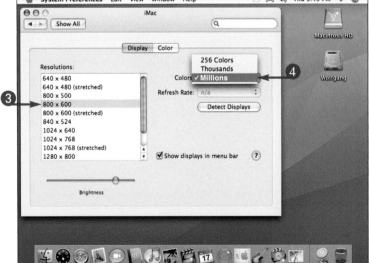

The Displays window appears.

③ Click the resolution that you want.

④ Click the Colors drop-down arrow and select the highest number of colors available.

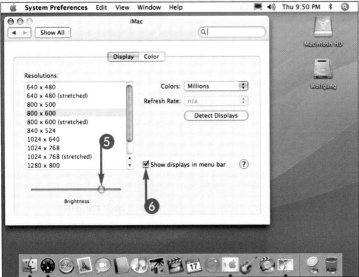

**5** Drag the Brightness slider to adjust the overall brightness of your display.

**6** Click the Show displays in menu bar to enable the check box (☐ changes to ☑).

*Note: This enables you to choose a resolution from the Mac OS X desktop menu bar.*

DIFFICULTY LEVEL

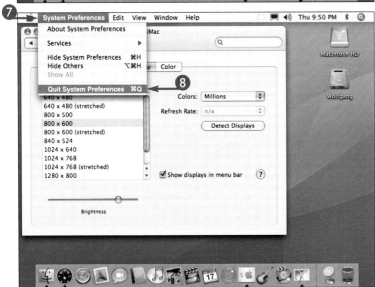

**7** Click System Preferences.

**8** Click Quit System Preferences to save your changes and close the System Preferences window.

## TIPS

### Did You Know?

In the Displays pane of the System Preferences window, if you click the Show displays in menu bar check box you can then click the Monitor icon in the Finder menu bar. A menu appears with the display resolutions you used recently. You can switch immediately by clicking the resolution that you want. You can also open the Displays pane from this menu.

### Did You Know?

CRT monitors typically use a specific refresh rate for each display resolution. Generally, the higher the refresh rate, the clearer the display; most computer owners also find a higher refresh rate causes less eyestrain. If you are using a flat-panel LCD monitor on your Mac, the Refresh Rate drop-down list in the Displays pane of System Preferences will be disabled.

# Display or hide
# DESKTOP AND SIDEBAR ICONS

You can configure your desktop and your Finder windows to provide as much or as little access to drives and external locations as you like. Tiger offers you the choice of hiding some of your Mac OS X desktop icons; you can also choose to display or hide most of the icons that appear in the sidebar of each Finder window that you open. If you want to help simplify your system for your kids or hide connected network servers from casual users, you are in the right place.

You can also specify the location shown within a new Finder window, including your home folder, your hard drive or your Documents folder. Choosing a new starting location can often save you two or three mouse clicks each time that you open a new Finder window.

To specify which icons appear on your desktop, use the settings on the General tab and the Sidebar tab within the Finder Preferences dialog.

① Click the Finder icon in the Dock.

The Finder window displays.

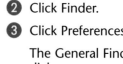

② Click Finder.

③ Click Preferences.

The General Finder Preferences dialog appears.

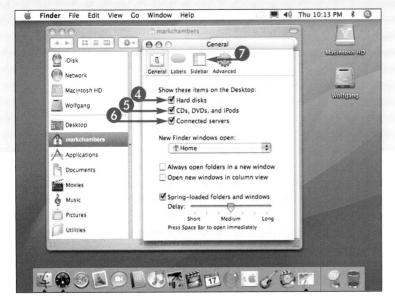

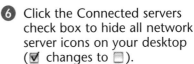

**DIFFICULTY LEVEL**

④ Under the General tab, click the Hard disks check box to hide all hard drive icons on your desktop (☑ changes to ☐).

⑤ Click the CDs, DVDs, and iPods check box to hide all CD, DVD, external hard drive, and Zip disk icons on your desktop (☑ changes to ☐).

⑥ Click the Connected servers check box to hide all network server icons on your desktop (☑ changes to ☐).

⑦ Click the Sidebar tab in the General Finder Preferences dialog.

The Sidebar Preferences dialog appears.

⑧ Click any of the drive or media items to hide all corresponding icons in the Finder window sidebar.

⑨ Click the Desktop, Home, or Applications check boxes to hide the corresponding locations in the Finder window sidebar.

⑩ Click the Close button to save your changes.

**TIPS**

### Customize It!

In the General Finder Preferences dialog, you can specify whether a new Finder window displays the contents of your Home folder or your computer when you first open it. If several people use the same Macintosh, the Home folder option is probably the best. If you are the only person using your computer, the Computer option is recommended.

### Did You Know?

Many Mac owners do not realize that an iPod can act as an external hard drive; by default, the iPod hardware icon appears on your desktop as soon as you connect your iPod to your Mac. However, if you have disabled the CDs, DVDs and iPods check box in the General Finder Preferences dialog, the iPod icon will not appear on your desktop.

# Customize your
# MOUSE AND KEYBOARD

You can fine-tune the behavior of your mouse and keyboard to match your personal preferences. In the world of the graphical user interface — or GUI, as it is commonly called — the mouse cursor is king, so it is important that your mouse's behavior match your preferences for things like double-clicking speed and tracking speed. And do not forget your keyboard: Because aftermarket keyboards are popular, you can also tweak your keyboard to match your typing style by adjusting settings like the rate at which keys repeat.

Even if you have been using Mac OS X for months now, you may find yourself returning to the Keyboard & Mouse pane in System Preferences when you buy a different mouse or replace your keyboard; generally, these new toys require a bit of adjustment before you are comfortable with them.

If you are using a wireless Bluetooth keyboard and mouse, you can also monitor their battery levels from within System Preferences.

1 Click the System Preferences icon in the Dock.

The System Preferences window appears.

2 Click the Keyboard & Mouse icon.

The Keyboard & Mouse window appears.

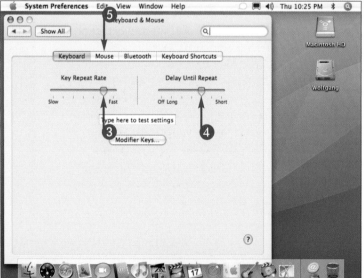

3 Under the Keyboard tab, drag the Key Repeat Rate slider to set the speed.

*Note: This slider controls how fast Tiger repeats a character when you hold down a key on your keyboard.*

4 Drag the Delay Until Repeat slider to set the speed.

*Note: This controls how long you must hold down a key on your keyboard before Tiger begins repeating the keystroke.*

To test the repeat rate and repeat delay, click in the Type here to test settings field and type.

5 Click the Mouse tab.

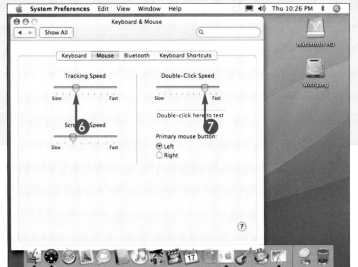

**6** Drag the Tracking Speed slider to set the speed.

*Note: This slider controls how fast your mouse pointer moves across your desktop when you move the mouse.*

**7** Drag the Double-Click Speed slider to set the speed.

To test the double-click setting, double-click in the Double-click here to test field. If some of the text is highlighted, you have set your Double-Click Speed slider correctly.

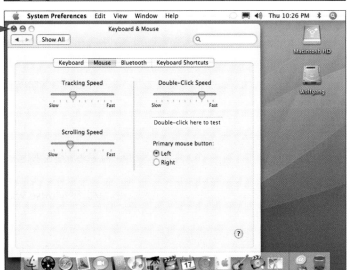

**8** Click the Close button to save your changes and close the System Preferences window.

### Customize It!
For precise work at the individual pixel level — such as image editing or desktop publishing — you may want to temporarily slow your mouse tracking to allow a finer level of control when you move your mouse. Conversely, most of today's fast-action 3-D games benefit from faster mouse tracking, as does the work you do in your everyday applications.

### Did You Know?
Tiger automatically detects whether or not your Mac includes Bluetooth networking hardware. If you do have Bluetooth installed, you will see the extra Bluetooth tab appear in the Keyboard & Mouse pane, as well as the Bluetooth icon within the System Preferences window. If you do not have Bluetooth hardware installed in your Mac, Tiger automatically hides these extra options.

# Change
# MENU COLORS

You can select the menu and highlight colors within Tiger to make them easier to see or more pleasing to your eye. There are two colorful decisions that you have to make when customizing the look of your Tiger desktop: You can set the Appearance color, which determines the coloring used in controls such as drop-down list boxes and buttons, and the Highlight color, which governs the color used when you highlight text in applications such as Word and Safari.

Besides the aesthetic improvement to your desktop, customizing these colors may help some visually

impaired Mac users recognize highlighted text and application or operating system controls more easily than they would with the default colors.

If you have switched to Tiger's reversed White on Black text option — using the settings in the Universal Access pane in System Preferences — these menu colors are disabled. The White on Black option is provided for those Mac users who have connected assistive devices, or Mac users who have trouble seeing the standard black on a white screen.

① Click the System Preferences icon in the Dock.

② Click the Appearance icon.

The System Preferences window appears.

The Appearance window of the System Preferences window appears.

③ Click the Appearance drop-down arrow and select Blue or Graphite.

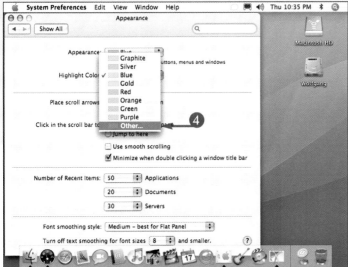

④ Click the Highlight Color drop-down arrow and select Other to specify your own highlight color.

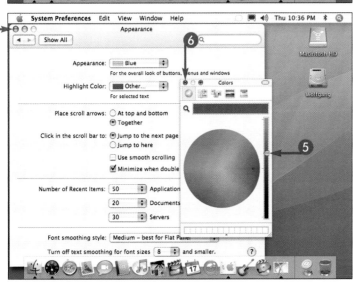

The Colors palette appears, in which you can click any color displayed in the wheel.

⑤ Click within the color wheel to set a color of your choice.

⑥ Click the Close button on the Colors palette.

⑦ Click the Close button to save your changes and close the System Preferences window.

## TIPS

### Customize It!

If you find the colors used within the Finder hard to see or hard to tell apart, consider using either Tiger's grayscale or white-on-black viewing modes, which can dramatically increase the contrast and readability of menus, windows, and dialogs. Both of these options are available on the System Preferences Universal Access pane. To set these features, refer to Task #4.

### Did You Know?

You can also fine-tune the readability of text within both your documents and the Finder. From the Appearances pane, click the Font smoothing style drop-down list and choose the Automatic option. If the text on your monitor still does not appear sharper, click the list and choose the Medium option for LCD monitors or the Standard option for CRT monitors.

# CHANGE DESKTOPS
## automatically

You can add variety and color to your desktop by setting Tiger to automatically switch your desktop background. Instead of manually changing the desktop background, you can *automatically* switch to a new desktop after a specified amount of time — without ever clicking a single control! You can even choose to rotate the display of images from a selected folder, or Tiger can surprise you and choose one at random.

You set up this feature using the Desktop & Screen Saver pane in System Preferences. Expect a certain

amount of disk activity and a pause of a few seconds when Tiger is busy changing your background. If you find this annoying, you can always configure Tiger to disable automatic background changes altogether.

Note that two other options are available for triggering a desktop background change: You can choose to switch backgrounds when you are logging in, which also works if you are using fast user switching, or Tiger can load a new background each time your Mac wakes from sleep mode.

❶ Click the System Preferences icon in the Dock.

The System Preferences window appears.

❷ Click the Desktop & Screen Saver icon.

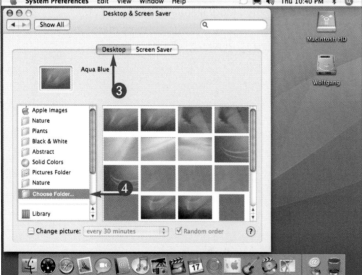

The Desktop & Screen Saver window appears.

❸ Click the Desktop tab.

❹ Click Choose Folder to select the source of the images.

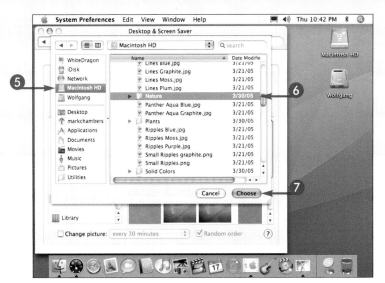

A File Open dialog appears.

**5** Click the source that holds the images you want to use.

**6** Click the folder that holds the images you want.

**7** Click Choose to display the pictures in the selected folder.

**8** Click Change picture to enable the check box (☐ changes to ☑).

Mac OS X enables the delay and random controls.

**9** Click the Change picture drop-down arrow and select the timing for which you want the background to change.

**10** Click the Close button to save your changes and close the Desktop & Screen Saver window.

---

**TIPS**

### Did You Know?

Tiger allows you to choose images from your iPhoto library for use as desktop backgrounds. At the bottom of the locations list on the Desktop pane, you will see a number of iPhoto locations, including your entire iPhoto library, all of your photo albums you have created, the last roll you imported, and even the last 12 months of images you have imported.

### Did You Know?

Some Macs feature widescreen LCD displays, which more closely match the proportions of a movie screen; many of today's televisions also offer widescreen display. Some background images take advantage of this widescreen aspect ratio — you can tell which images are widescreen by their appearance in the scrolling thumbnail display. Standard aspect backgrounds appear square, while widescreen backgrounds appear as longer rectangles.

# Chapter 2

# Managing Files and Folders

The Finder has always been one of the most important aspects of the Mac OS. After all, this one often-copied feature set the Mac apart from its competition back in the early days of the personal computer. Tiger continues in this tradition with Finder features that help make your file management much quicker and easier. For example, every Finder window has a Sidebar that gives you extraordinarily speedy access to nearly any location on your hard drive. You can display information about any file or folder on your hard drive using the Get Info command from the Finder menu, or by using the keyboard shortcut.

Color labels make it easier to locate the documents for a specific project, or arrange your files according to your deadlines. You can create an alias for any application, allowing you to launch that application from different locations on your hard drive. You can also configure Tiger to automatically encrypt the contents of your Home folder using the FileVault feature in System Preferences, preventing anyone else from opening documents or viewing the images you have stored in your Home folder.

New in Tiger is the Spotlight menu, conveniently available from the Finder menu. Unlike the more traditional file and folder Search features offered in the Finder window and through the ⌘–F shortcut key, Spotlight enables you to search for specific information throughout your entire system, including your Apple Mail messages, iCal events, and Address Book entries.

# Top 100

# Accelerate file access with Tiger's
# FINDER SIDEBAR

Beginning with Mac OS X 10.3, or Panther, Apple made some significant changes to the Finder, including a number of improvements to the Finder window itself. Each Finder window has a Sidebar that displays drives, including hard drives, removable drives, such as CD and DVD, network drives, and even your iDisk. You can view the contents of any drive by clicking its icon in the Sidebar; the drive's contents appear in the Content view. As you navigate through the folders on a drive, the Sidebar remains constant. When you change between Icon, List, and Column views, the Sidebar does not change.

You can customize the area below the drives in the Sidebar with your own files and folders. As you add an item to the Sidebar, the icons in the sidebar resize to accommodate the new addition until you reach the icons' minimum size.

Removing items from the Sidebar is a simple drag-and-drop operation. When you drag items away from the Sidebar, they disappear completely. If you have ever removed items from the Dock, you will be at home with this operation.

1 Click the Finder icon in the Dock.

A new Finder window appears if one was not already present.

2 Click a drive icon in the Sidebar to view its contents.

3 Drag a drive icon in the Sidebar to rearrange its position in the sidebar.

The other drive icons move to accommodate the new drive position.

4 Select a view type for the window by clicking one of the three View icons.

The Sidebar continues showing your drives and custom elements and the Content view changes.

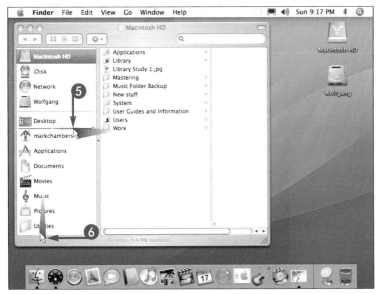

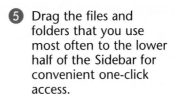

⑤ Drag the files and folders that you use most often to the lower half of the Sidebar for convenient one-click access.

The Sidebar icons resize to accommodate the new additions.

⑥ Drag the icons at the bottom of the Sidebar to arrange them to your whim.

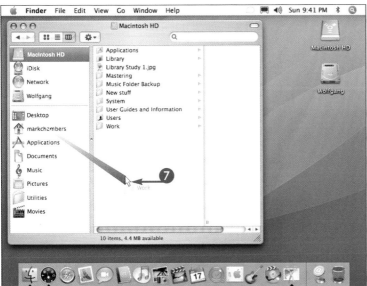

⑦ Drag an icon from the bottom of the Sidebar to anywhere outside of the sidebar.

The icon is removed from the Sidebar.

## TIPS

### Did You Know?

Removing an icon from the Sidebar has no effect on the item that it represents. Removing a document from the Sidebar does not delete the actual file or move it to the Trash. It simply removes the item from the Sidebar. Items in the Sidebar work somewhat like aliases. If you remove one, you can always re-create it later.

### Did You Know?

The Sidebar is an optional aspect of the Tiger Finder. If you prefer the Finder style of older Mac operating systems, simply drag the vertical handle beside the Sidebar to the left. When the handle meets the left edge of the window, the Sidebar disappears, giving you additional room to display icons, list details or columns depending on your view mode.

# Leverage
# KEYBOARD SHORTCUTS
## to speed up work

You can customize the default keyboard shortcuts within both Tiger and many applications to make your Mac easier and faster to use. Despite the ease of use that you gain from a mouse, sometimes using a keyboard is faster. To this end, Mac OS X Tiger includes all kinds of useful keyboard shortcuts. The base key for keyboard shortcuts is the Command key. In addition to the Command key, keyboard shortcuts often use other modifier keys such as Option and Shift. Using the Command key and some other combination of keys, you can perform nearly every operation on your Mac without ever touching the mouse.

The Finder is one of the biggest supporters of keyboard shortcuts. You can find many of these shortcuts by reading the shortcuts displayed in each menu of the Finder.

In addition to the default keyboard shortcuts available in the Finder and other applications, you can also create your own custom keyboard shortcuts via the Keyboard pane of the System Preferences dialog box.

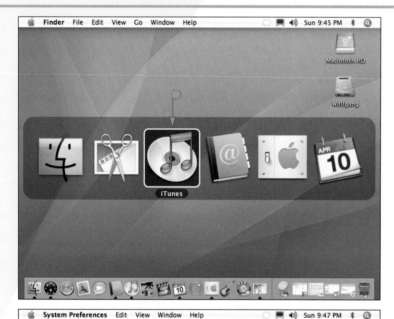

### TOGGLE BETWEEN DOCK APPLICATIONS

1 Press ⌘–Tab to switch to the last open application you used.

2 Press and hold ⌘ and repeatedly press Tab to cycle through each of the open applications.

● The application-switching window appears with the active application highlighted.

3 Press ⌘–Shift–Tab to switch the applications in the opposite direction.

### OPEN DIFFERENT SYSTEM PREFERENCES PANES

1 Press Option and one of the speaker buttons on the keyboard.

The Sound pane opens within the System Preference window.

2 Press Option and either F15 or F14 on the keyboard.

The System Preferences window switches to the Displays pane.

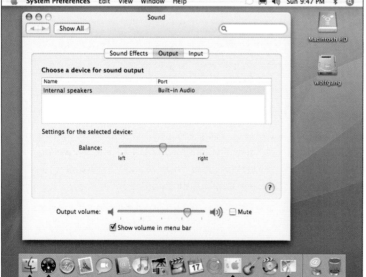

28

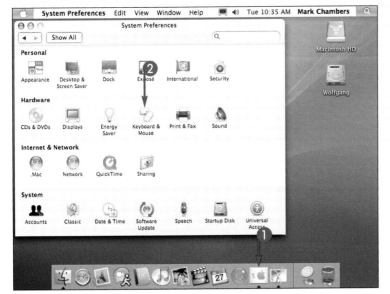

1 Click the System Preferences icon in the Dock.

The System Preferences window appears.

2 Click Keyboard & Mouse.

**DIFFICULTY LEVEL**

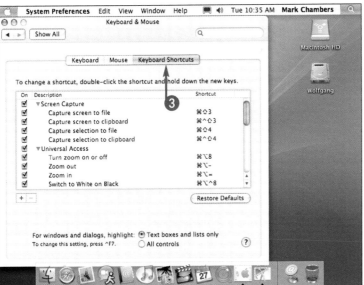

The Keyboard & Mouse pane appears.

3 Click Keyboard Shortcuts.

The Keyboard Shortcuts section of the Keyboard & Mouse Preferences pane appears, where you can change your keyboard shortcut settings.

## Customize It!

You can really hot-rod your Mac like never before with the custom keyboard shortcuts in the Keyboard Shortcuts pane of System Preferences. It is here where you can toggle premade keyboard shortcuts on and off. You can also change the keyboard combinations that make the shortcuts function. Furthermore, by clicking the Add Keyboard Shortcut button, you can create your own keyboard shortcuts.

## Did You Know?

New Macintosh keyboards lack a Power key, as was in vogue for years on Macintosh keyboards. This does not mean, however, that you cannot still use your keyboard to shut down as when the keyboards did have Power keys; you can press Control–Eject to make the standard Shutdown window appear. However, to start up your Mac, you are still relegated to pushing the button on the machine itself.

# COPY FILES
## four different ways

You can use the Finder to copy files and folders from location to location within Tiger quickly and easily; in fact, copying files is so important that the Mac OS gives you four different ways to do it. Whether you choose to use the keyboard shortcut, the contextual menu's Duplicate item, the mouse and keyboard shortcut, or the Copy, Edit, and Paste menu items, copying files is vital for making backups, experimenting with a file without ruining it, and other tasks.

In addition to the specific copying tasks, the Finder sometimes copies automatically for you. For example, if you drag a file from one disk to another, the Finder assumes that you want to make a copy on the destination drive. On the other hand, if you drag a file from one place on a drive to another location on the same drive, the Finder moves the file; no copy operation takes place.

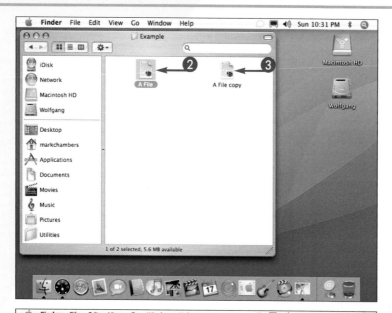

### USE A KEYBOARD SHORTCUT

① Open a Finder window and navigate to a file or folder that you would like to copy.

② Select the file or folder by clicking it.

③ Press ⌘–D.

The Finder creates a copy of the file in the same location as the original.

### USE THE CONTEXTUAL MENU

① Control–click a file or folder that you would like to copy.

A contextual menu appears over the file or folder.

② Click Duplicate.

Alternatively, you can click File→Duplicate.

The Finder creates a copy of the original file or folder in the same location as the original.

## USE THE OPTION KEY AND DRAGGING

① Press and hold the Option key.

② Drag the file that you would like to copy to a destination location.

The Finder creates a copy of the file in the destination that you designated.

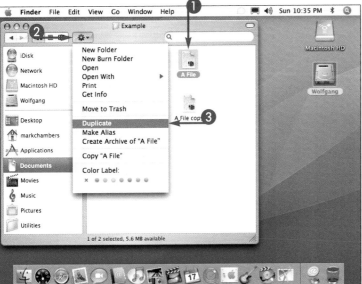

## USE THE ACTION MENU

① Click a file or folder that you would like to copy.

② Click the Action menu.

③ Click Duplicate.

The Finder creates a copy of the original file or folder in the same location as the original.

 TIPS

### Apply It!

All the copy operations described in this task work for one file or multiple files. To copy multiple files to the same location, first select them in the Finder and then perform a copy operation by Option–dragging, copying via the contextual menu, or pressing ⌘–D.

### Did You Know?

Everyone makes mistakes, and the Finder can compensate for that. The Undo function works in the Finder to help you out of jams: If you make a mistake, press ⌘–Z. The Finder immediately undoes any damage you may have done. This is handy for times when you accidentally copy files to the wrong location.

# CREATE AN ALIAS

You can open documents and launch applications from any folder on your hard drive by using aliases. Sometimes simply hunting down a commonly used file or folder is inconvenient. To make your life easier, the Mac OS gives you aliases. *Aliases* are special files that do not do anything except point to another file or folder. They are not copies of the file or folder. They have only one purpose: to show you where a file is. Rather than dig through folders looking for a file that you use all the time, you can create an

alias for it and place that alias somewhere convenient, such as on your desktop or in the Favorites folder. Then, when you want to open that file or folder, all you have to do is double-click its alias.

Aliases can also reveal the location of the file or folder they represent. This is especially handy for locating the original file and navigating to the location of that file very quickly.

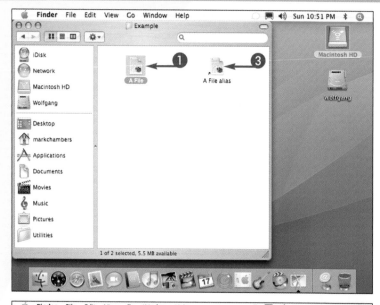

### USE A KEYBOARD SHORTCUT

1 Click to select a file or folder in the Finder.

2 Press ⌘–L.

The Finder creates an alias that points to the file or folder.

3 Move the alias to someplace convenient for easy access to the original file or folder.

### USE A MENU

1 Control–click a file or folder in the Finder.

A contextual menu appears.

2 Click Make Alias.

Alternatively, you can click File→Make Alias.

The Finder creates an alias for the file or folder.

3 Drag the newly created alias to the location that you want.

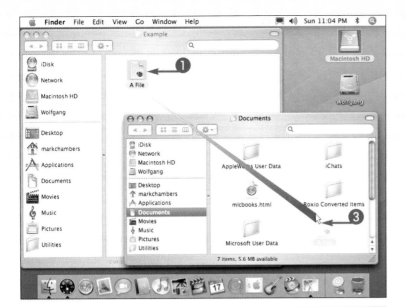

## Use Keys and Dragging

1. Click to select a file or folder in the Finder.

2. Press and hold the ⌘–Option keys.

3. Drag the file or folder to a new location.

   The Finder creates an alias to the file in the destination of your choice.

**DIFFICULTY LEVEL**

## Locate an Alias's Target File or Folder

1. Locate an alias in the Finder.

2. Control–click the alias.

   A contextual menu appears.

3. Click Show Original.

   A Finder window opens showing the location of the original file or folder that the alias represents.

### Did You Know?

Aliases are superintelligent and can actually fix themselves whenever possible. You can safely move the file or folder that an alias points to without breaking the link between them. Instead of pointing to a specific location, an alias tracks the original file it points to in much the same way that you track a car with a GPS device.

### Apply It!

Besides the usual aliases in the Finder window, the Dock has its own aliaslike functionality. Click and hold an application icon, or right-click the icon, to reveal a Show in Finder contextual menu item. This Dock feature can be especially useful if you want to navigate quickly to that application's parent folder.

# PROTECT FILES
## from prying eyes

You can securely encrypt the files and folders stored within your Home folder, protecting them from other users, by enabling FileVault. Tiger includes a very powerful security feature called FileVault, which protects your files with string encryption.

FileVault encrypts all files contained within your Home directory, using a top-notch encryption routine that is hard for anyone to decode. You will not even notice that the encryption is taking place because Tiger performs that operation while you use the file. Later, when you want to open a protected file, Tiger

decrypts it and opens it automatically once again in the background, invisible to you. You can access your encrypted files as long as you are logged in as a valid user.

If you forget your personal password, which is your login password, you cannot retrieve your files; however, you can set a master password that will unlock FileVault. An Admin account is required to set the master password within the System Preferences window.

**SET YOUR MASTER PASSWORD**

① Click the System Preferences icon in the Dock.

② Click Security.

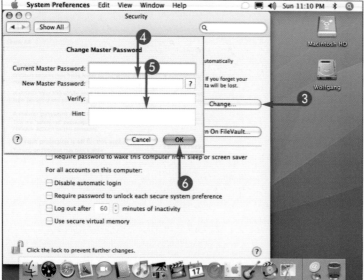

The Security pane appears.

③ Click Change.

The Change Master Password dialog appears.

④ Type the password.

⑤ Type a hint to remind you about the password.

⑥ Click OK.

The master password is set.

1 Click the System Preferences icon in the Dock.

2 Click Security.

**DIFFICULTY LEVEL**

The Security pane appears.

3 Click Turn On FileVault.

Tiger prompts you for a password.

4 Type the password.

Tiger displays a confirmation dialog.

5 Click Turn On FileVault to enable encryption.

As soon as you turn on FileVault, Tiger logs you out and begins encrypting your Home directory. After it is encrypted, you can log in again and return to your work.

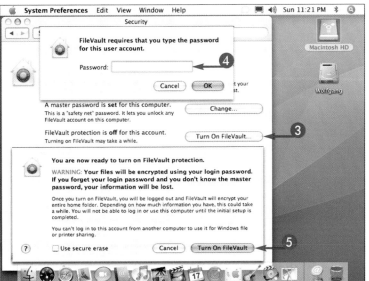

## Apply It!

File encryption is particularly useful for laptop owners. If you lose your laptop, you can at least be certain that no one will be able to read your important business and personal documents; however, you must set Tiger's login feature to require a password. To do this, make sure the Disable automatic login box is unchecked on the Security pane.

## Did You Know?

When FileVault is active, your Home folder is displayed as a silver house icon sporting a vault lock. Tiger uses the same type of 128-bit encryption that is commonly used by the government and the military, which means that a common hacker will have an incredibly hard time breaking through the security protecting the files and folders stored within your Home folder!

# FIND FILES AND INFORMATION
## in a flash

You can quickly search through all of the thousands of files on your Mac's hard drive for specific text using Tiger's new Spotlight technology.

Macintosh operating systems have always been good at helping you find files on your hard drive. Tiger's new Spotlight feature takes a giant leap forward, offering nearly instantaneous searches that include just about any type of information on your system: files, images, PDF documents, messages from Apple Mail, contacts from your Address Book, and even events from your iCal calendars! With Spotlight, you

are not just searching through file names, but through the actual content within those files.

The Spotlight search box is available directly from the Finder menu bar, allowing you to search for information from wherever you are in the Finder. Of course, you can always use the traditional Search window by pressing the Command key and the letter F. Spotlight technology is also used within the System Preferences window, to allow you to search for settings using words like "screen saver" or "desktop background."

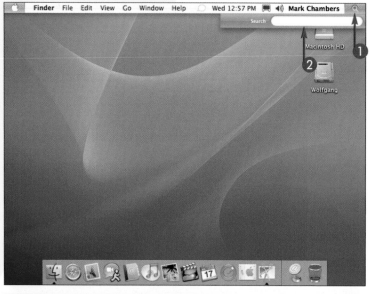

### USING SPOTLIGHT TO SEARCH YOUR SYSTEM

**1** Click the Spotlight icon at the far-right side of the Finder menu bar.

Tiger displays the Spotlight search box.

**2** Type some text in the Search field.

Your Mac begins searching for files, folders, and information the second you press a key. As you continue typing, the search further refines itself based on what you have typed.

**3** Click one of the matching entries in the Spotlight hit list.

Tiger displays the desired file, folder, or document. If the match is a document, the corresponding application is automatically launched and the document is loaded.

USING THE SEARCH
DIALOG BOX

① Click File.

② Click Find.

Tiger displays the Search dialog.

③ Type some text in the Search field.

Your Mac begins searching for files and
folders while you type. As you continue
typing, the search further refines itself
based on what you have typed.

④ Click one of the matching entries in the
Search results list.

Tiger displays the desired file or folder.

*Note: The Search dialog is used to locate
only files and folders that match your
search text.*

### Did You Know?

Spotlight can actually search for text
embedded within a PDF file, so it is no
longer necessary to open a PDF
document within Preview to check it for
a specific phrase. If you have a large
number of software and hardware
manuals in PDF format on your hard
drive, you can use Spotlight to help you
troubleshoot problems by searching for
text from error messages!

### Did You Know?

The search/find functions in the first
version of Mac OS X used to appear
in the Sherlock application. They
no longer appear there, as Sherlock
has become solely an Internet tool
since Mac OS X 10.2. In Tiger,
Sherlock is more useful in tracking
down information like maps, AppleCare
topics, movies being shown in your
area, and stock quotes.

# Access file information with
# GET INFO

You can display all sorts of information about specific files and folders by using Tiger's Get Info command. Finder windows give you a lot of information about files and folders, but they reveal only a fraction of what is possible. By opening the Get Info window for a file or folder, you can learn about and alter a variety of information.

The Get Info window displays information about files and folders contextually, which is to say that it displays specific data depending on what the file or

folder is. You can view and change all sorts of information about a file or folder, including its name, size, type, date modified, date created, file extension, icon, permissions, and comments.

You can also lock a file to protect it from being changed by anyone, including yourself within the Get Info window. Although you can still open or launch a locked document or application, locking a file ensures that you will not send it to the Trash by accident.

① In the Finder window, select a file or folder by clicking it.

② Click File.

③ Click Get Info.

The Get Info window opens.

④ Click a disclosure triangle to expand that portion of the Get Info window.

⑤ Click the Ownership & Permissions disclosure triangle to see which users can read and write to the file or folder.

If you have an appropriate account, you can change the permissions for the file or folder.

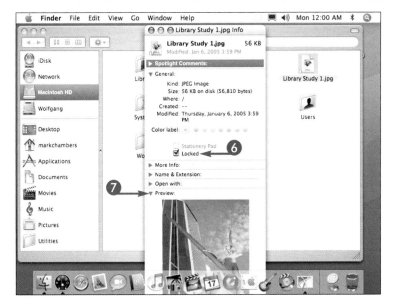

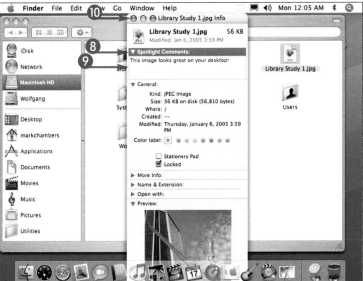

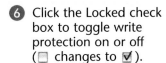

#17

DIFFICULTY LEVEL

**6** Click the Locked check box to toggle write protection on or off (☐ changes to ☑).

If a file or folder is locked, it cannot be deleted from the Trash.

**7** Click the Preview disclosure triangle to display a preview of a file's contents.

If the contents of the file can be readily displayed, like an image or a text file, a thumbnail view appears in the Preview section.

**8** Click the Spotlight Comments disclosure triangle.

**9** Click within the Comments field and type to enter comments on the selected file or folder.

**10** Click the Get Info window Close button.

## TIPS

### Caution!

Be very careful if you change permissions on a file or folder; otherwise, another user may not be able to use it later, or the application associated with the file may not work at all. Changing permissions on files requires a user with the appropriate rights to do so. You can also verify and repair the permissions on a disk using Tiger's Disk Utility.

### Did You Know?

You can also display the Get Info window to check on the total capacity and the remaining free space on any drive on your Tiger desktop, including both internal and removable hard drives. Even an iPod, a CD-ROM or DVD-ROM you have loaded will display much of the same information whenever you select them and use the Get Info command.

# USE COLOR LABELS
## to prioritize your files

You can organize and prioritize your files and folders in Tiger by using color labels. Labels offer a set of colors that you can attach to a file or folder to denote your own form of colorized organization, or to prioritize files according to their importance or due date.

Suppose, for example, that you would like to sort all of the files in a particular folder based on how important they are to your employer. Your Mac cannot distinguish the importance of one document

you have over another file. By using labels, you can assign a scale of importance to your files that is reflected in their color. After you have assigned an importance to each of the files, sorting them visually by that importance is a quick and straightforward matter. You can also arrange files by color if you are using the Finder's icon view mode.

You can use labels to identify files and folders by their associated projects, or by the deadlines that each file or folder is due.

### LABEL WITH A CONTEXTUAL MENU

① Open a Finder window that has files and/or folders in it that you would like to sort.

② Control–click the file or folder.

A contextual menu appears.

③ Under Color Label, click a color to represent some criterion for the file.

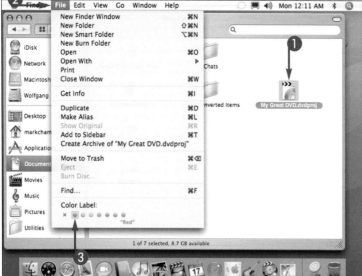

### LABEL WITH THE FILE MENU

① In a Finder window, click to select a file or folder.

② Click File.

③ Click a color under Color Label to change the color for the file or folder.

The file or folder is now labeled with the color that you specified.

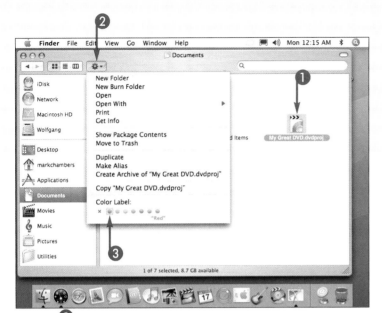

LABEL WITH THE ACTION MENU

1. In a Finder window, click to select a file or folder.

2. Click the Action menu.

3. Click a color under Color Label to change the color for the file or folder.

   The file or folder is now labeled with the color that you specified.

ARRANGING FILES BY LABEL IN ICON MODE

1. Click the Finder icon in the Dock.

2. Click File.

3. Move your mouse pointer over the Arrange menu item.

   Tiger displays the available arrangement choices.

4. Click Label.

## TIPS

### Did You Know?

For years, Macintosh users were accustomed to sorting their files in the Finder by name, date, type, and label. However, Mac OS X 10.0 through 10.2 lacked the label feature, resulting in a wave of complaints from long-time users. Panther reintroduced labels in a new-and-improved form, and they continue to appear in Tiger, where you can once again sort files by label.

### Did You Know?

You can change the names associated with each label color from the Finder Preferences dialog. Click Finder, click Preferences, and then click the Labels tab. Click within the text box next to each color and type the new name. When you are done, click the Close button on the Finder Preferences dialog to return to the Finder.

# OPEN A FILE
## with an alternate application

You can load your documents in your favorite applications by specifying which application will automatically launch for a particular file type. When you double-click a file in the Finder, an application usually launches that can handle that type of file. This works fine for most day-to-day tasks, but sometimes it is not what you want.

Suppose, for example, that you have a JPEG file that you downloaded from the Internet using Safari. Perhaps all your JPEG icons display an icon based on the Preview application. When you want to edit the

image that you downloaded with another application such as Adobe Photoshop CE or Photoshop Elements, you usually have to jump through some hoops to make the image open in the other application.

Fortunately, Tiger takes away some of the guesswork. You can instantly change which application will open a specific type of file. You can also tell your Mac to open all files of that type with the application of your choosing.

### CHOOSING AN APPLICATION FROM THE CONTEXTUAL MENU

1 Click the Finder icon in the Dock.

Tiger opens a new Finder window; if you already have a Finder window open, it becomes active.

2 Control–click the desired file to open a contextual menu.

3 Position your mouse over Open With.

Tiger displays a submenu with all of the applications that are capable of opening that type of document.

4 Click the desired application.

Tiger launches the application and automatically loads the document.

CHOOSING AN ALTERNATIVE APPLICATION

① Click the Finder icon in the Dock.

Tiger opens a new Finder window; if you already have a Finder window open, it becomes active.

② Control–click the desired file to open a contextual menu.

③ Position your mouse over Open With.

④ Click Other.

The Choose Application dialog opens.

⑤ Select an application.

⑥ Click Open.

---

## Did You Know?

The steps outlined in this task may not be necessary for some file types. That is because an application that you have installed has already done the job of associating itself with the file type for you during the installation process. Double-clicking any file of that type will now launch the third-party application instead of the Tiger default application.

## Did You Know?

If you are certain that you want a specific application to always open this type of file, click the Always Open With check box, in the Choose Application dialog, to enable it ( ☐ changes to ☑ ). Tiger will now launch with the application you selected every time you open a file of that type.

# CUSTOMIZE ICONS
## for files and folders

You can customize your file and folder icons by copying them from other documents and applications on your hard drive. As has been the case for years through many different versions of Mac OS X, you can customize the icon of any file or folder in the Finder. Icons are vital components of the Mac's graphical user interface, even if you do not use Icon view in the Finder. They help you quickly identify files and folders without having to read a filename, making it much easier to tell what application will

launch or what action will take place when you load a particular document.

Many items on your hard drive have uniquely identifiable icons, and many software developers produce applications with sets of icons that include templates, macros, AppleScripts, and even the application folder itself. To those items that do not, however, you can assign a custom icon; this will continue to save you time far into the future.

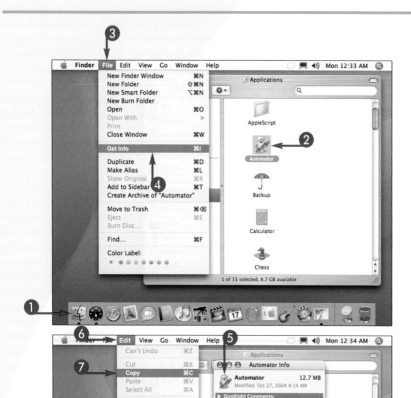

1 Click the Finder icon in the Dock.

2 Choose a file or folder in the Finder whose icon you would like to use.

3 Click File.

4 Click Get Info.

The Get Info window opens.

5 Click the icon at the top of the Get Info window.

6 Click Edit.

7 Click Copy.

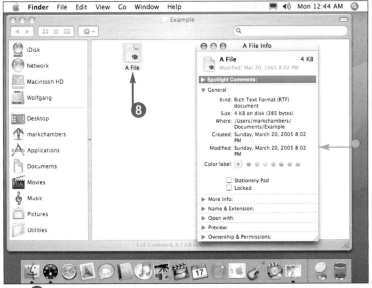

8 Click a file or folder in the Finder whose icon you would like to change.

9 Press ⌘-I.

● Tiger opens the Get Info window for the file or folder.

10 Click Edit.

11 Click Paste.

12 Click the Get Info window Close button.

## Did You Know?

Although it is perfectly okay to copy icons among the files on your Mac's hard drive for your own personal use, attaching those icons to files that you have created for distribution to others is not allowed. In fact, many software developers have actually copyrighted the symbols incorporated into their icons. If you are distributing your own Automator application or Dashboard widget, you do not have to design a new icon.

## Did You Know?

Customizing an icon for a document does not change the document's file type within Tiger, so the application that will launch when you double-click that file remains the same. Only the image used for the icon is modified. Likewise, copying an icon for an application does not change the document icons for new documents that you create with that application.

# Chapter 3

# Using Your Desktop More Efficiently

A car may actually have only three basic controls — a steering wheel, brake pedal, and accelerator pedal — but how you *use* those controls makes a big difference! It is the same with the basic controls within Mac OS X. Anyone can use the Dock to launch or switch between applications, but the desktop contains hidden power that can also help you work more efficiently with Tiger and your applications. The same holds true for keyboard shortcuts, the Finder window, and the Go menu.

One new feature in Tiger deserves a special mention: the Dashboard, which can display an entire screen's worth of miniapplications (or widgets) with a single press of a function key. Common widgets on your desktop may include a calculator, a stock ticker, a world time clock, and a video player. In this chapter, you will find out how to use this great efficiency feature.

This chapter demonstrates some of the tricks that can help you speed through your daily tasks on your Macintosh. You will find tips on adding your favorite applications, items, and Web sites to the Dock, as well as how to resize the Dock and move it to a new position on your desktop. This chapter also covers how to set your Mac to start or shut down automatically at certain times, and how to allow other users to access your computer without you needing to log out.

# Top 100

# Add and delete
# DOCK ICONS

You can customize the Dock to display the applications and documents that you use most often. You can even remove the default icons for applications that you seldom need; if you do not use the iTunes or iCal applications every day, why allocate space for them in the Dock? With a few seconds' work, you no longer have to open a Finder window or create an alias on your desktop to enjoy quick and easy access to the tools that you need throughout a computing session.

To save even more time, you can perform certain application commands right from the Dock. Many applications offer a Dock menu from which you can access the most important functions of that application (often without displaying the application window). A good example is Apple's DVD Player, which offers a full set of player controls from the Dock menu. Other Dock menu items can display the application in a Finder window, or hide the application window.

ADD A DOCK ICON

① Drag the item's icon from the Finder window to the Dock.

The icon is added to the Dock.

REMOVE A DOCK ICON

① Drag the icon from the Dock and drop it anywhere on your desktop.

The icon is removed from the Dock.

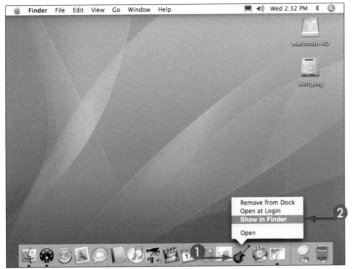

## SHOW A DOCK ITEM IN THE FINDER

① Click an icon in the Dock and hold down the mouse button.

**Note:** *You can also hold down the Control key while you click, or click the right mouse button if you have one.*

Tiger displays the Dock contextual menu.

② Click Show in Finder.

Tiger opens a new Finder window showing the location of the item.

## EMPTYING THE TRASH FROM THE DOCK

① Click the Trash icon in the Dock and hold down the mouse button.

Tiger displays the Empty Trash contextual menu.

② Empty Trash.

Tiger empties the Trash.

DIFFICULTY LEVEL

---

### TIPS

#### Did You Know?
You can add a folder to the right side of the Dock — the portion of the Dock to the right of the vertical line. To view the contents of a folder, click and hold down your mouse button on top of the folder icon. You can then click to launch any item in the pop-up menu.

#### Did You Know?
Some Dock icons can display more than just the Show in Finder, Remove from Dock, and Open at Login items on the pop-up menu. The commands available on the pop-up menu vary between applications, so make sure you try the click-and-hold trick for every application you use. Some commands are actually available only under certain conditions, and may be disabled at other times.

# Customize the
# FINDER TOOLBAR

You can add and remove controls from the Finder window toolbar, making it easy to arrange the Finder contents for maximum efficiency. Because the Finder window is the most often-used tool in Tiger, customizing its controls is usually a good idea. Available controls that you can add to the default control group include common functions like Get Info, Search, Delete selected items, and Eject. You can also access your iDisk, connect to a server, or record a CD or DVD using the Finder toolbar.

By using the space, flexible space, and separator icons, you can group your Finder window toolbar icons into whatever arrangement suits you best. For example, you can add a space followed by a separator and the Delete icon. Because you do not want to delete any selected items accidentally, the combination of the space and the separator help keep the Delete icon at a safe distance from the other controls.

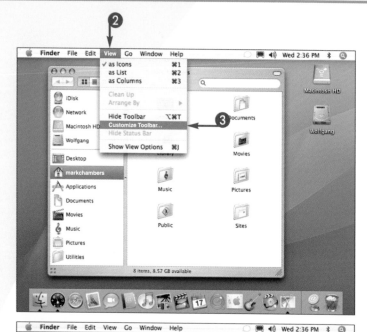

① Press ⌘-N.

Tiger displays a new Finder window.

② Click View.

③ Click Customize Toolbar.

Tiger displays the Customize Toolbar dialog.

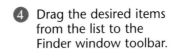

DIFFICULTY LEVEL

④ Drag the desired items from the list to the Finder window toolbar.

A rectangle appears to indicate where the item can be placed, and existing icons will move automatically.

To remove an item, drag it from the toolbar to the desktop.

⑤ Click the Show pop-up menu and click Icon Only to turn off toolbar labels.

⑥ When you have finished modifying the toolbar, click Done.

Your changes appear on the toolbar.

TIPS

## Customize It!

You can choose to display just text labels on your Finder toolbar. In the Customize Toolbar dialog, click the Show drop-down arrow and select Text Only. Using only text labels instead of icon graphics greatly reduces the size of the Finder toolbar, allowing Tiger to display more icons or list items in a Finder window.

## Customize It!

If you would rather not eliminate the icon graphics in the Finder toolbar, you can reduce their size and still save space for icons and list items. In the Customize Toolbar dialog, click to enable the Use Small Size check box. Tiger reduces the icons in size by approximately 50 percent, leaving more space in the Finder window.

# RELOCATE AND RESIZE
## the Dock

You can customize the Dock's position and size by adjusting the Dock settings in System Preferences. For example, you are not required to put the Dock at the bottom of the desktop; if you prefer, you can move the Dock to the right or left side of the desktop. This is especially helpful when running applications that fill the entire vertical height of the screen, like AppleWorks; by moving the Dock to the left side of the desktop, you can extend your application window into that space at the bottom of the screen.

You can also change the size of the icons in the Dock whenever you want, and you can resize the Dock to accommodate the addition of a larger number of icons. Tiger even enables you to hide the Dock completely until it is needed, or to magnify a dock icon when you position the mouse over the icon.

① Click the System Preferences icon in the Dock.

The System Preferences window appears.

② Click Dock.

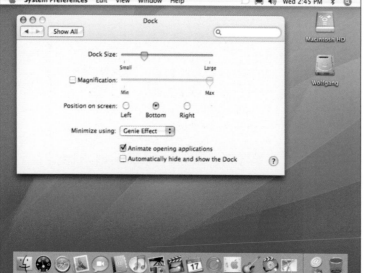

The Dock settings appear.

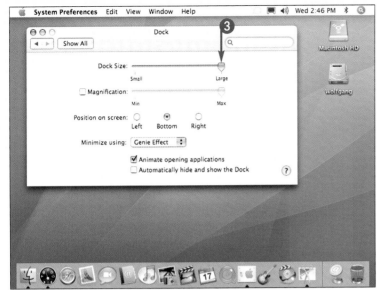

③ Drag the Dock Size slider to resize the Dock icons.

④ Click Left, Bottom, or Right to specify where the Dock should appear (○ changes to ⦿).

⑤ Press ⌘-Q to quit System Preferences and save your changes.

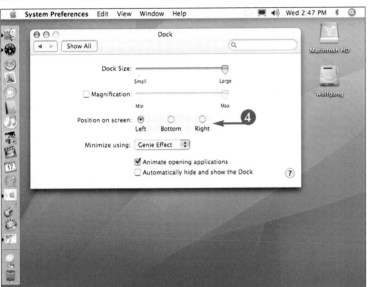

## TIPS

### Did You Know?

You can elect to hide the Dock entirely by clicking to enable the Automatically hide and show the Dock check box in the Dock pane of System Preferences. The Dock disappears, but you can display it again by moving your mouse cursor all the way to the edge of the screen where the Dock previously appeared.

### Customize It!

You can configure dock icons to *magnify* — temporarily expand in size — when your mouse pointer hovers over them. This makes choosing the correct icon much easier. Click the Magnification check box, and then drag the slider to specify the magnified size. To turn magnification off, click the Apple menu and click the Dock menu item, and then click Turn Magnification Off.

# CUSTOMIZE EXPOSÉ
## for keyboard or mouse operation

Tiger's Exposé feature is designed to make switching between application windows much easier, especially when you are running a large number of applications simultaneously. You can control the feature through keyboard shortcuts, mouse buttons, and activation/deactivation *corners* that you specify in System Preferences. If you activate hot corners, then moving your mouse cursor to the specified corner activates the chosen Exposé command.

By default, you can display all of your application windows at one time by pressing the F9 key; click

a particular window to activate it. To display only the active windows for the current application, press and hold F10 and then click on the window that you want. Press and hold F11 to move all application windows to the edges of the screen, enabling you to work with items on your desktop. Finally, you can activate Dashboard by pressing F12 once to display the Dashboard menu or by holding F12 to display your Dashboard widgets.

**①** Click the System Preferences icon in the Dock.

The System Preferences window appears.

**②** Click Dashboard & Exposé.

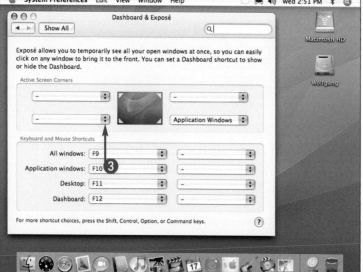

The Dashboard & Exposé settings appear.

**③** Click the drop-down arrow for the corner that you want to set.

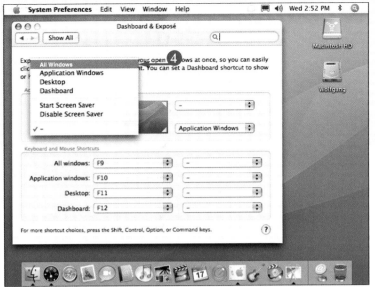

④ Click the menu command that you want to assign to that corner.

*Note: For example, selecting All Windows displays all of the windows when you move your mouse cursor to that corner.*

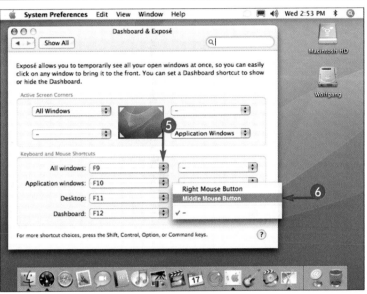

⑤ Click the top three Keyboard drop-down arrows to specify new Exposé keyboard shortcuts.

⑥ Click the top three Mouse drop-down arrows to specify new Exposé mouse button assignments.

⑦ Press ⌘–Q to quit System Preferences and save your changes.

## Did You Know?

You can also use screen corners to turn on (or disable) your screen saver. The same set of screen corner command options appear in both the Dashboard & Exposé pane and the Desktop & Screen Saver pane. Configuring the screen corners in one System Preferences pane automatically updates the options in the other pane.

## Did You Know?

You can use the Shift, Control, Option, and ⌘ keys in conjunction with Exposé keyboard shortcuts and mouse button assignments to access a far greater range of combinations. To use one of these modifier keys, click on the Exposé control you want to configure and press the desired modifier key. The entries in the list box change immediately to include the modifier key!

# PUT YOUR MAC TO SLEEP
## to save energy

You can conserve electricity and reduce the heat your Mac generates by switching on sleep mode. Many Mac owners tend to turn off their computers each time they leave their desks. This makes good sense if you are leaving for several hours (as in a daytime office job); but if you will return in a few minutes, or even an hour or two, putting your Mac into sleep mode instead is much more efficient. Laptop owners should take advantage of sleep mode whenever possible, since sleep mode can help conserve battery power; closing the screen on most Mac laptops triggers sleep mode.

Besides the benefits of energy conservation and keeping your computer cool, you will also save time if you put your Macintosh in sleep mode rather than turning it off: Tiger takes far less time to return from sleep mode than to start up. Although any running applications pause while your system is asleep, they resume without problems when your Mac returns from sleep mode.

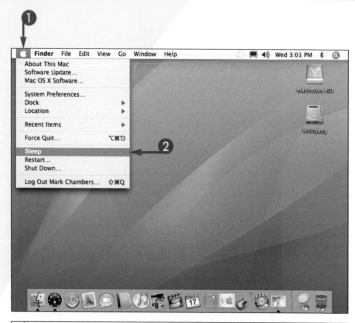

**PUTTING YOUR MAC TO SLEEP FROM THE APPLE MENU**

❶ Click  .

❷ Click Sleep.

Your Mac's screen blanks.

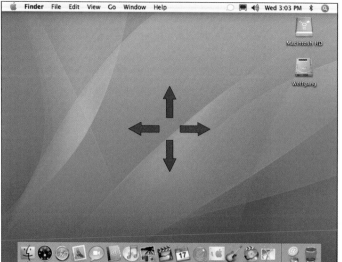

❸ To wake up your Mac, press any of the arrow keys on the keyboard.

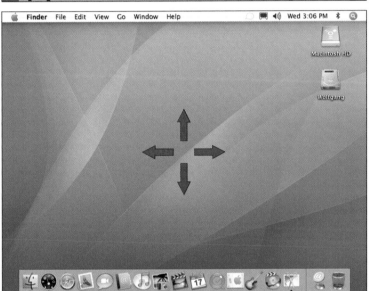

## PUTTING YOUR MAC TO SLEEP FROM THE KEYBOARD

1 Press and hold the Control key while pressing the Media Eject key.

   *Note: The Media Eject key is located in the upper-right corner of most Apple Pro keyboards.*

   A confirmation dialog appears.

2 Click Sleep.

   Your Mac goes to sleep.

3 To wake up your Mac, press any of the arrow keys on the keyboard.

## TIPS

### Did You Know?

You can set your Mac to automatically enter Sleep mode from System Preferences. Open the Energy Saver pane and click the Sleep button. Drag the Put the computer to sleep slider to the desired delay. Your Mac enters Sleep mode when the delay period passes without any activity. To turn off Sleep mode entirely, move the slider to Never.

### Did You Know?

Most new Macintosh models have a visual indicator to help you determine when the computer is in Sleep mode; for example, the power light on the iMac G5 pulses slowly whenever the computer is in sleep mode. You can always safely check to see if your Mac is sleeping by pressing one of the arrow keys.

# SWITCH BETWEEN USERS
## without logging off

You can share your Mac more efficiently between multiple users by enabling Tiger's fast user switching feature. If you share your Mac with others — perhaps in a home, an office, or a classroom environment — you have likely been stuck sitting idle while another user finishes a session. (And all you really needed was 5 minutes of time on the computer!) Older versions of Mac OS X allowed only one user to log in to the computer at a time, forcing other users to wait until that person completely logged off.

With Tiger's fast user switching feature, you can log in even if someone is already logged in with another account — perhaps to just print one of your documents, copy a file into your Shared folder, or quickly check your e-mail. When you are finished with your tasks, you can log off and the original user can switch back to his or her session, without losing any documents or shutting down any applications.

① Click the current user name on the Finder menu.

Tiger displays the User Switch menu.

② Click the account name to which you want to switch.

Tiger prompts you for the new user's login password (if a password is required).

**DIFFICULTY LEVEL**

3 Type the password.

4 Click Log In.

Tiger logs in the new user and displays that person's desktop.

**TIPS**

### Try This!

To toggle fast user switching, use an Admin-level account to open System Preferences. Open the Accounts pane, click the Login Options button, and click the Enable fast user switching check box to enable or disable this feature. Tiger displays the current user at the right side of the Finder menu whenever fast user switching is turned on.

### Caution!

Although you can shut down or restart while logged in via fast user switching, the original user will lose any unsaved documents. Therefore, it is a good idea to check the User Switch menu to determine whether others are logged in before shutting down or restarting. Mac OS X displays a check mark next to any active accounts.

# START OR SHUT DOWN
## your Mac automatically

You can easily configure your Macintosh to automatically start whenever you like; your computer can be ready and waiting for you when you reach your home or office! You can also leave your Mac on when you go out, since Tiger can actually turn your Macintosh off for you at a specific time. Using your Mac's built-in clock, Tiger can start up or shut down most Macintosh computers automatically at a regular schedule.

If your Macintosh is in a secure location where other people cannot use it — like your locked office — you can combine this automatic start feature with Tiger's capability to automatically log in a specific account and launch login items for that account. After everything is configured, you can walk into your office every morning and be greeted with Word, iSync, iCal, and Apple Mail already running! All the settings you need to fine-tune are available from the Energy Saver and Accounts panes within System Preferences.

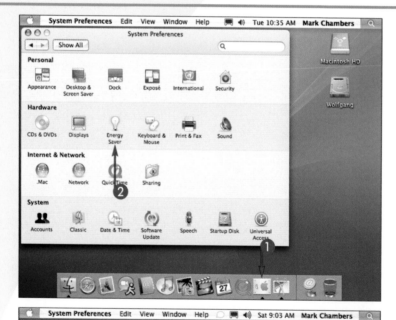

① Click the System Preferences icon in the Dock.

The System Preferences window appears.

② Click Energy Saver.

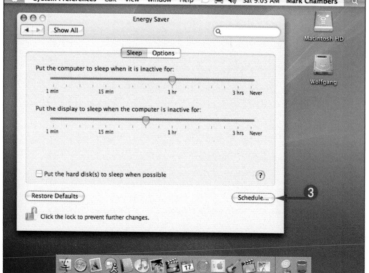

The Energy Saver settings appear.

③ Click Schedule.

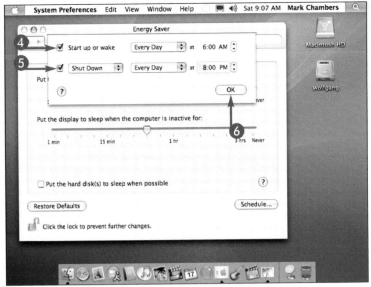

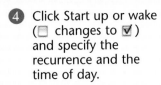

④ Click Start up or wake (☐ changes to ☑) and specify the recurrence and the time of day.

⑤ Click the second check box and select (☐ changes to ☑), Shut Down, and then specify the recurrence and the time of day.

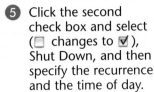

**DIFFICULTY LEVEL**

⑥ Click OK.

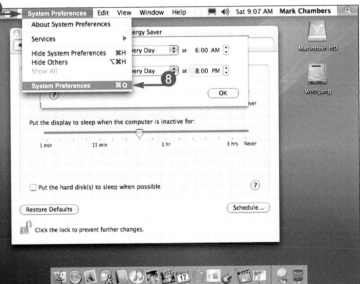

⑦ Click System Preferences.

⑧ Click Quit System Preferences to close the window and save your changes.

---

## TIPS

### Did You Know?
By default, your Macintosh remains off if you are hit by a power failure. However, you can specify that Tiger should restart your Mac automatically once power is restored after a power failure. From the Energy Saver pane, click the Options button, and then click to enable the Restart automatically after a power failure check box.

### Caution!
Make sure that your Mac is in a secure location before you set both automatic start up and automatic log in. Anyone walking up to the computer will have read and write access to your Home folder and all of your application data — like your Mail messages — after your Mac has powered up.

# ADD WEB SITES
## to the Dock

You can add your favorite Web sites to the Dock, which will save you time and eliminate several mouse clicks every time you want to visit one of those sites. Instead of launching the Safari Web browser separately and clicking the Web site in the Bookmarks list, a Web icon in the Dock simplifies the entire process to a single click by automatically launching Safari and loading the page.

Web sites added to your Dock appear with an @ icon; by hovering your mouse pointer over the icon, you

can see the name of the linked Web page. When you click the @ icon, Tiger automatically launches your Safari browser, connects to the Internet if necessary, and loads the site. You may have noticed that the default Dock arrangement already includes a Web site: Clicking this Dock icon jumps right to the Mac OS X main page on Apple's Web site at www.apple.com.

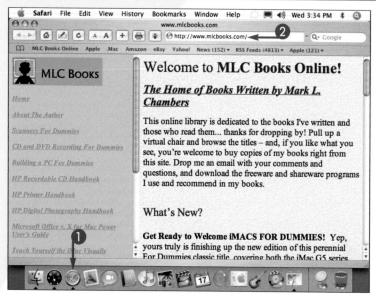

① Click the Safari icon in the Dock.

The Safari window appears.

② Navigate to the Web page that you want.

③ Drag the URL icon from the Address bar to the right side of the Dock.

Tiger adds the Web page to the Dock.

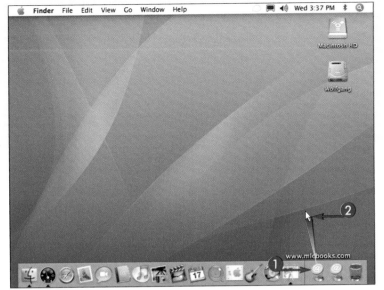

## REMOVING A WEB SITE FROM THE DOCK

① Click a Web icon in the Dock.

② Drag the icon from the Dock to the desktop.

The mouse pointer turns into a "puff of smoke."

③ Release the mouse button.

The Web page icon disappears.

## TIPS

### Did You Know?

When you minimize a Safari window, a miniature thumbnail of the Web page appears in the Dock. If the page is updated by the Web server — like www.cnn.com or other news sites — the thumbnail also updates to reflect the change. To return the window to its original position so you can read the new content, click the page thumbnail in the Dock.

### Customize It!

Adding the Web page for Apple's Tiger Support to your Dock is a good idea; that way, you are never more than a single click away from online help with Tiger. If your Dock is short on space, you can remove the default Web page icon that takes you to the top-level Mac OS X page.

# Save time with
# KEYBOARD SHORTCUTS

You can customize the global keyboard shortcuts used throughout Tiger, making it easier to remember and use those common shortcuts wherever they appear. The global keyboard shortcuts work the same in all applications and for all sorts of operating system commands and actions. (Because Apple has subtly changed the standard Macintosh keyboard layout from model to model, most Mac old-timers have used this trick at least once: They have changed a new keyboard shortcut to match the old shortcut they have been using for years.)

Even if this is your first Macintosh and you are just starting to learn the common shortcuts, you may want to change a specific default keyboard shortcut because you find it hard to remember or difficult to use; or you may decide to add an entirely new keyboard shortcut that better suits your needs. You can make your changes to these keyboard shortcuts from the Keyboard & Mouse pane within System Preferences.

① Click the System Preferences icon in the Dock.

The System Preferences window appears.

② Click Keyboard & Mouse.

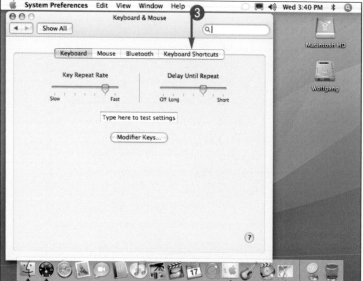

The Keyboard & Mouse settings appear.

③ Click Keyboard Shortcuts.

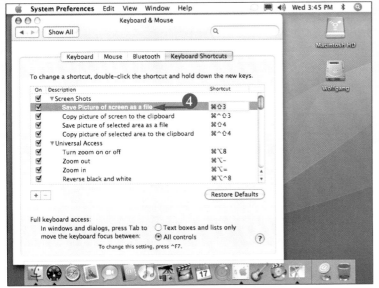

④ Double-click the shortcut you want to change.

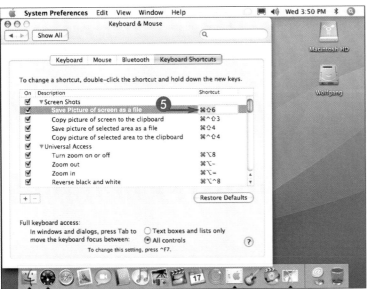

⑤ Press the new key shortcut.

⑥ Press ⌘–Q to quit System Preferences and save your changes.

## Customize It!

To add a new keyboard shortcut, click the plus (+) button in the Keyboard Shortcuts pane. Choose the target application that will recognize the new shortcut, and type the menu command that the shortcut will trigger. The command name must be spelled exactly as it appears in the menu. Click in the Keyboard Shortcut box, type the new shortcut, and click Add.

## Did You Know?

It is also possible to control your Macintosh without touching it! You can use the built-in speech recognition features in Tiger to launch applications, control editing functions, and perform common tasks. Open the System Preferences window and click Speech to enable the Speakable Items system. To toggle listening mode on, hold down the Esc key while speaking commands.

# UTILIZE DASHBOARD
## to handle simple tasks

You can add *widgets* to your display with Dashboard — a new feature in Tiger — and use them to perform common functions throughout your day. A widget is a small applet that typically performs a single function, like a clock or a calendar. Widgets load quickly and do not take up a lot of room on your hard drive like larger applications. New widgets are offered for downloading on the Apple Web site.

Like Exposé, Dashboard is controlled from the keyboard, the mouse, or screen corners. In fact,

you configure your Dashboard key combination from the Dashboard & Exposé pane in System Preferences, so the two features are tied closely together. When you press the Dashboard key, the widgets appear, ready for you to use. You can drag new widgets to your Dashboard from the menu. Press the Dashboard key again or click any open area on the screen to return to your Tiger desktop. (You can also click the Dashboard icon in the Dock to toggle the Dashboard display.)

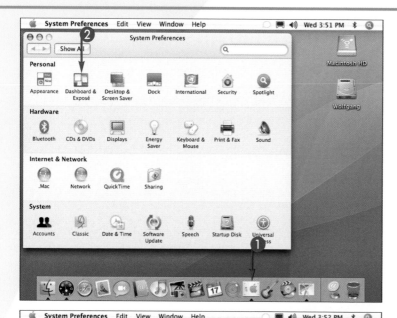

**①** Click the System Preferences icon in the Dock.

The System Preferences window appears.

**②** Click Dashboard & Exposé.

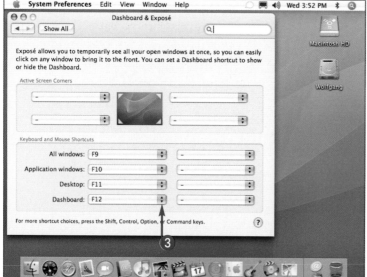

The Dashboard setting appears.

**③** Click the Dashboard drop-down arrow.

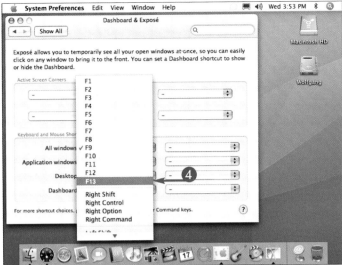

④ Click the function key that you want to assign to Dashboard.

**DIFFICULTY LEVEL**

⑤ Click the Close button to close System Preferences and save your changes.

## Did You Know?
The Mac OS X site has additional widgets that you can download — visit Apple's Mac OS X page at www.apple. com/downloads/macosx/dashboard/ to choose from the latest widget offerings. Third-party software developers also offer widgets for downloading; some are free and others are shareware, which you can try out first and then purchase if you like.

## Did You Know?
Like Exposé key combinations, you are not limited to just the keys listed in the Dashboard drop-down menu. Use the Shift, Control, Option, and ⌘ keys in conjunction with the Dashboard key to specify a modifier. Click the Dashboard drop-down arrow, press the desired modifier key, and then click the modified key combination from the list.

# Expanding Your Mac's Horizons

You are no longer a newcomer to Tiger. You have mastered the basics of using the Finder, connecting to the Internet, launching applications, and manipulating windows.

Now it is time to raise the bar by moving on to some of the more advanced features within Mac OS X: tricks that enable you to stay organized, protect your personal information, communicate with other devices, and even control your Mac with your voice. You may not need to use these features during each computing session, but they can really deliver in certain situations. For example, you may not have to create a PDF document every day; but when you need to offer a long document for downloading on your Web site, Tiger's Save As PDF feature comes in very handy!

This chapter provides tips and tricks for experienced Mac OS X users, covering a wide range of topics throughout Tiger. You will find demonstrations on how to reveal the UNIX command prompt, how to enhance data security with FileVault and Secure Empty Trash, and how to boot from a specific operating system. This chapter also includes information on connecting with portable devices using iSync, and shows you how to add new fonts to your system. If you need a little organization in your business and personal life, you can find out how to use Stickies to jot simple notes and how to add an event or appointment in iCal. You also learn about Tiger's powerful voice command feature, which activates an entirely new method of operating your computer.

# Top 100

# CONNECT
## to other devices with iSync

You can use Tiger's iSync application to exchange iCal calendar data and Address Book contacts between your Macintosh and your iPod; and you can expand this group by exchanging information between Mac OS X and many cell phones, laptops, printers, and PDA units. Many of these portable devices now use Bluetooth, a new short-range wireless technology that is now built into many Macintosh desktop and laptop computers.

You must first connect a portable device to your Mac — using a wired connection, such as USB,

FireWire, or a wireless connection with Bluetooth — before you can follow the steps in this task. You may also have to install the driver software provided by the device's manufacturer. You can tell that most of these devices have been successfully connected if they appear on your Tiger desktop or within a Finder window. Bluetooth devices that have successfully linked to your computer should appear in Tiger's Bluetooth menu in the Finder menu.

① Click the Finder icon in the Dock.

Tiger opens a new Finder window.

② Click Applications in the Sidebar.

③ Double-click iSync.

- The iSync window appears.

④ Press ⌘–N.

- iSync displays the Add Device dialog.

⑤ Double-click the device that you want to use.

**DIFFICULTY LEVEL**

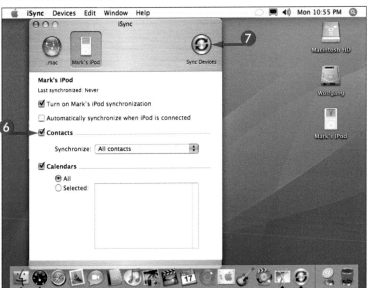

The iSync window expands to show you what data can be synchronized.

⑥ Click the check boxes for the data that you want to exchange (☐ changes to ☑).

*Note: For example, with an iPod connected, you can copy your Mac OS X Contacts and Calendar data.*

⑦ Click Sync Devices.

## TIPS

### Did You Know?

After you have added a device, iSync automatically recognizes that device whenever you run the application. Of course, you must connect to the device first. Bluetooth devices usually need to be set as discoverable in order to link automatically. You can plug FireWire and USB devices into your Mac at any time, but you must eject them (like a DVD) before they can be removed.

### Warning!

Never disconnect a device while using iSync. Breaking the connection before iSync completes the transfer may result in corrupted or lost data on the portable device, and can actually cause iSync to lock up. If iSync does lock up, you can use the Force Quit feature under the Apple menu to manually quit the application.

# USE STICKIES
## on your desktop for quick reminders

You can use Tiger's Stickies application to store important things like addresses, images, and quick reminders on your desktop. Although the name is a little silly, Tiger's Stickies mimic paper sticky notes, enabling you to place multiple notes for yourself anywhere on your desktop. For example, you can use a Stickies note to hold snippets of text or an image from a Web site until later in the day, when you can import the text or graphic into an AppleWorks document.

Stickies notes make great reminders, and they can even help you stay organized. You can make Stickies windows translucent or different colors to help you determine their priority. Stickies share many of the features of a text editor or word-processing application: You can print the contents of the active note, search for a specific string of text, export text to a file on your hard drive, and even include graphics by dragging the images into the note window.

① Click the Finder icon in the Dock.

Tiger opens a new Finder window.

② Click Applications in the Sidebar.

③ Double-click Stickies.

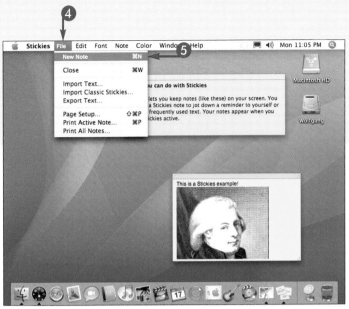

Your existing Stickies appear.

④ Click File.

⑤ Click New Note.

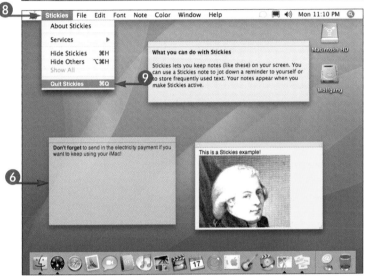

⑥ Type the contents of the note.

*Note: You can format your text with ⌘–B (bold), ⌘–I (italic), and ⌘–U (underline).*

⑦ To save all open Stickies, press ⌘–S.

⑧ Click Stickies.

⑨ Click Quit Stickies to exit.

### Did You Know?

Notes remain stuck to your desktop for as long as the Stickies application is running. However, like other Mac applications, you can hide all the notes on your desktop by using a File menu command, click Stickies, and then click Hide Stickies. To return the notes to the desktop, click the Stickies application icon in the Dock.

### Customize It!

If you find that you use Stickies often, you can launch the Stickies application automatically each time you log in. Open System Preferences, click Accounts, and click your account to select it. Click the Login Items button and click the Add button ( + ) at the bottom. Select the Stickies application, and then click Add.

# Access UNIX with
# TERMINAL

You can access the UNIX core within Tiger by using the Terminal application. Mac OS X is stable, reliable, and fast due to its UNIX foundation; but unless you use the Terminal application, you will never see the UNIX command line. If you want to type UNIX commands, or you would like to handle an FTP session the old-fashioned way, use Terminal to launch a UNIX command-line session.

When you first launch Terminal, your current directory is your Home folder — a convenient place to start if you want to edit a document.

Many freeware and shareware applications — typically called *front-end* applications — have been written to provide a more user-friendly, point-and-click means of controlling the most popular UNIX programs available through the Terminal application. It is always worth a Google search to see whether a UNIX program has a Mac OS X front end available. If not, you need to open Terminal and type the commands directly, as shown in this task.

① Click the Finder icon in the Dock.

Tiger opens a new Finder window.

② Click Applications in the Finder.

③ Double-click the Utilities folder.

④ Double-click Terminal.

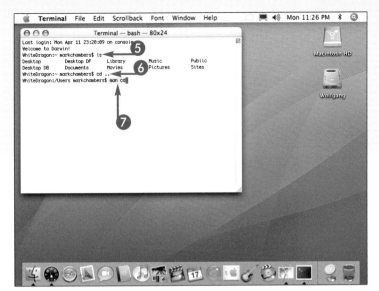

The Terminal window appears.

⑤ To display the contents of the current directory, type **ls** and press Return.

⑥ To change to the parent directory of the current directory, type **cd ..** and press Return.

⑦ To display help information for any command, type **man <command name>** and press Return.

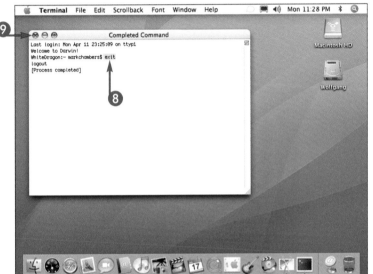

⑧ To quit Terminal, type **exit** and press Return.

Terminal logs you out.

⑨ Click the Close button.

## TIPS

### Did You Know?

Mac OS X Tiger ships with a collection of UNIX programs, including the Apache Web server, FTP, the Sendmail e-mail server, and the Emacs text editor. If you are interested in learning UNIX, pick up a copy of a good UNIX book, such as *UNIX For Dummies,* 4th Edition, by John R. Levine and Margaret Levine Young (also from Wiley Publishing).

### Warning!

Some commands available from the Terminal command line can erase files and folders, change permissions on applications and data files, or produce problems with the system files that form the foundation of Tiger. Therefore, make sure that you fully understand the correct syntax for every command you try, as well as the results that command will produce.

# Delete your
# TRASH SECURELY

You can use the Secure Empty Trash command to ensure that the items in your Trash are beyond recovery. When you empty your Trash by clicking Finder and then Empty Trash, or with the ⌘–Shift–Delete keyboard shortcut, you may think that the contents are gone forever; however, that is really not true. You can still read those files using a third-party disk utility such as Norton SystemWorks, and the data can be restored.

If you are working with sensitive or personal data that needs to be erased permanently, use the

Secure Empty Trash menu command. This command overwrites the contents of the Trash several times with random data and prevents those files from being restored in the future. If you have several large files in your Trash — for example, a number of video clips or high-resolution photos — Secure Empty Trash takes a little longer than Empty Trash. But if security is an issue, those extra seconds are well worth the wait.

① Click Finder.

② Click Secure Empty Trash.

The Secure Empty Trash confirmation dialog appears.

③ Click OK.

Your Trash is deleted securely.

ELIMINATING THE WARNING
WHILE EMPTYING THE TRASH

1 Click Finder.

2 Click Preferences.

The Finder Preferences dialog appears.

3 Click Advanced.

4 Click the Show warning before emptying the Trash option (☐ changes to ☑ ).

5 Click the Close button on the Preferences dialog.

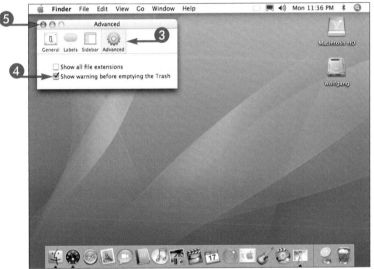

**TIPS**

### Did You Know?

Folders and files that you have moved to the Trash remain there until you use one of the two Empty Trash commands. To restore a file from the Trash, simply click the Trash icon in the Dock to display the contents, and then drag the folders or files that you want to recover back to their original locations.

### Did You Know?

You can empty the Trash directly from the Dock with just your mouse. Click and hold the mouse while hovering over the Trash icon in the Dock. A pop-up menu appears. Click Empty Trash. Note that the Empty Trash Securely method is not available from the Trash icon in the Dock. You can also choose to Open the Trash from this menu.

# Protect your privacy with
# FILEVAULT

You can use Tiger's FileVault feature to secure the contents of your Home folder so that no other user can open or display the contents of the folder. If you are sharing your Macintosh with other users, you may be concerned about securing the documents, folders, and files in your Home folder against prying eyes. Tiger's FileVault feature protects your Home folder by encrypting its contents, using industrial-strength encryption routines that make it virtually impossible for anyone to access your files without your password.

Your FileVault password is your login password, so a successful login automatically gives you access to your Home folder; you will not even know file encryption is active. However, before you can turn on FileVault protection for your account, an admin-level user must set the FileVault master password. This password can unlock any of the Home folders encrypted with FileVault on your Mac, making it a great safety net in case a user forgets a login password.

① Click the System Preferences icon in the Dock.

The System Preferences window appears.

② Click Security.

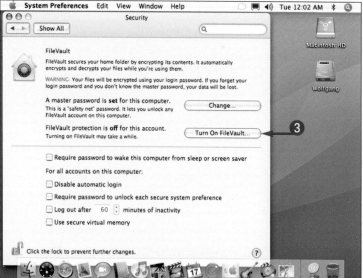

The Security settings appear.

③ Click Turn On FileVault.

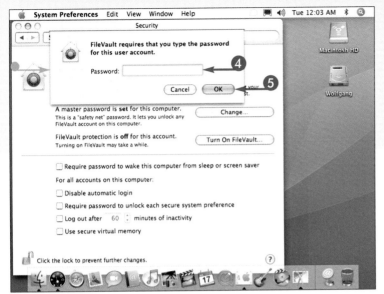

● Tiger displays a password dialog.

④ Type your account's login password.

⑤ Click OK.

# 35
DIFFICULTY LEVEL

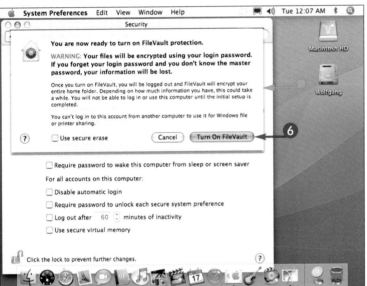

● Tiger displays a confirmation dialog.

⑥ Click Turn On FileVault.

Tiger shuts down all running applications and displays an encryption progress dialog.

After encryption is complete, you can log in normally.

TIPS

## Caution!

If you forget your login account password and an admin-level user cannot provide the correct master password on the Security pane in System Preferences, the contents of your Home folder are lost *permanently;* the encryption cannot be removed without one of these passwords. Even Apple technical support representatives cannot help you if you forget your FileVault passwords!

## Caution!

Make sure that you have closed any open documents before you enable FileVault protection for your Home folder; save the documents first and quit out of the applications before you begin the steps provided in this task. Otherwise, you could lose any changes you have made to your documents when Tiger automatically shuts down to begin the encryption process.

# START APPLICATIONS AUTOMATICALLY
## when you log in

You can use Tiger's Login Items feature to automatically launch any number of applications as soon as you log in to Mac OS X. This is a great feature if you find yourself running the same set of applications each time you log in, like Mail, Pages and iCal. Tiger launches any applications specified as Login Items as soon as your desktop appears, so you may notice a slight delay before you can use your Mac.

You can even specify the order in which the applications run, which may be necessary if one application requires another application to be running. You can also specify whether your Login Item application windows appear on the desktop when they are launched or start up in hidden mode. Note, however, that the current user can only modify the Login Items assigned to his or her account, so your Administrator cannot set up Login Items for you. You have to log in with your own account to complete this task.

① Click the System Preferences icon in the Dock.

The System Preferences window appears.

② Click Accounts.

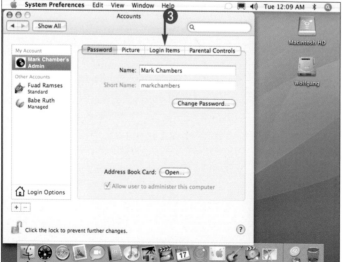

The Accounts settings appear.

③ Click Login Items.

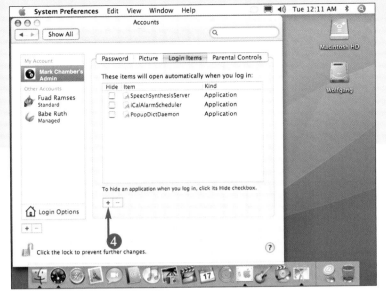

④ Click the Add button.

Tiger displays an Open dialog.

⑤ Navigate to the desired application and double-click it.

⑥ Press ⌘–Q to quit System Preferences and save your changes.

## TIPS

### Did You Know?

You can run a Login Item hidden in the background by enabling its Hide check box in the Login Items list of the System Preferences Accounts pane. When Tiger launches the application, the application window will not appear on the desktop. To display the application window, click on the application icon in the Dock.

### Did You Know?

To remove an application from the Login Items list of the System Preferences Accounts pane, select the application in the list and click the Remove button ( – ). To change the order in which Login Items are launched, click and drag the entries to the desired order in the list.

# ACTIVATE VOICE COMMANDS
## to speak to your Mac

The voice control system of your Mac recognizes spoken commands, which many Mac users find faster than using the mouse. The fact that virtually all current Macintosh models come equipped with a built-in microphone is no accident: Tiger's voice control system, which you can activate within System Preferences, allows your Mac to perform all sorts of chores via voice commands. Voice control requires proper inflection and rhythm, and it does take some time to learn. Although controlling your computer

with your voice is not as precise as using your mouse and keyboard, you may find that supplanting your keyboard and mouse with voice commands can help you operate your Mac more efficiently.

Those Mac owners who find using the mouse difficult will also find voice control very helpful, especially because Tiger includes commands for many common tasks like closing a window, opening Mail, and quitting an application. You can even ask Tiger to tell you a joke!

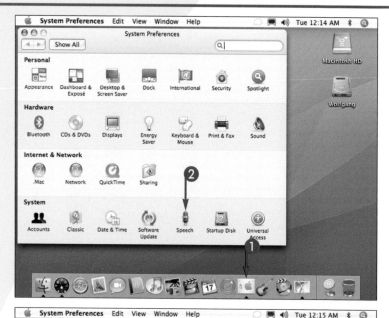

① Click the System Preferences icon in the Dock.

The System Preferences window appears.

② Click Speech.

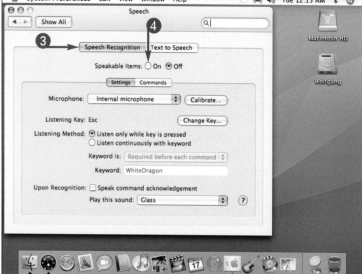

The Speech pane appears.

③ Click Speech Recognition.

④ Click On (○ changes to ◉ ).

The round Speech window appears.

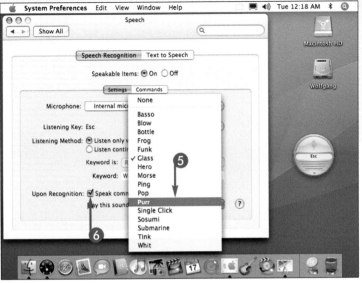

5 Click the Play this sound drop-down arrow to select an acknowledgement sound.

6 Click Speak command acknowledgement (☐ changes to ☑).

7 Click System Preferences.

8 Click Quit System Preferences.

You can now press Escape and speak a voice command.

## TIPS

### Customize It!

Tiger begins to monitor your voice when you hold down the Escape key, and stops monitoring when you release it. You can change this on the Settings panel of the Speech pane in System Preferences. Click the Change Key button to specify a new key. Instead of pressing a key, you can choose a keyword that is spoken before each command.

### Did You Know?

To view the default spoken commands that Tiger will understand, click the Commands button on the Speech pane, and then click the Open Speakable Items Folder button. Tiger displays the contents of the folder; each file name represents a spoken phrase. You can also enable and disable spoken command sets for many applications (like Address Book) and menu bars.

# Save documents as
# PDF FILES

You can use the standard Print dialog to produce PDF (Portable Document Format) documents with Tiger's built-in PDF creation feature. Third-party applications like Adobe Acrobat are well-known PDF creation tools, but these applications are generally very expensive and have dozens of features that you may never use. As long as you can print from an application, Tiger can do the job for you, producing a PDF document that you can send in e-mail or offer as a download on your Web site.

PDF documents can be opened and viewed on-screen by any computer that can run Adobe's free Acrobat Reader (available at www.adobe.com); so PDFs are a great way of distributing documents to users on different platforms, such as Linux and Windows. A PDF file can also be printed, enabling users to produce hard copies of the document if necessary. PDF documents can contain embedded images — just insert them into a document as you normally would — and Tiger can customize your finished PDF file with the page settings you specify.

① Open the document that you want to make into a PDF.

② Click File.

③ Click Print.

Alternatively, you can press ⌘–P.

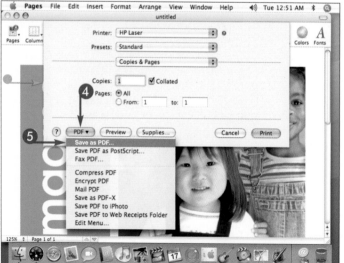

● The standard Print dialog appears.

④ Click PDF.

⑤ Select Save as PDF.

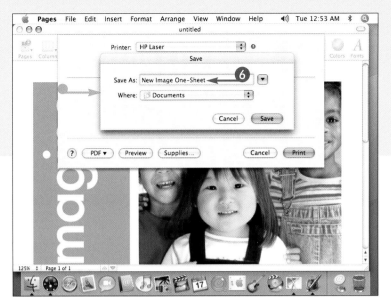

● The Save to File dialog appears.

⑥ Type the file name.

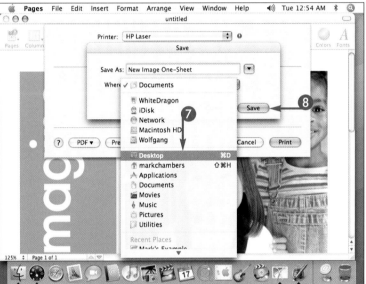

⑦ Click the Save As drop-down arrow and select the target location.

⑧ Click Save.

Tiger saves the document as a PDF.

## Did You Know?

You can use the settings of the Page Setup dialog to adjust the orientation and scale of your document before you create the PDF. Note that other settings may also be available to customize your finished PDF document, depending on the application; for example, you can also modify the margins if you are using Microsoft Word.

## Did You Know?

Tiger uses the Preview application to display PDF files that you download from the Internet or create with your own applications. Preview is a fast performer, and enables you to navigate through a PDF document using page thumbnails, zoom in and out, or rotate the entire image (useful for those documents that contain graphics in landscape orientation).

# Configure your personal
# ADDRESS BOOK CARD

You can select a specific Address Book card for your user account, allowing Tiger and many applications to automatically enter your personal information within e-mail messages, faxes you send, and Web sites you visit. Your card contains information like your telephone number, mailing address, and e-mail addresses, as well as your company information. This special card is identified as your Personal card, or "My Card," and you can change it at any time.

Tiger identifies your Personal card with a special label, and you can add a picture as well. Tiger's

Address Book application can produce a vCard file for your Personal card, which you can then attach to your e-mail messages or share with others who use contact databases.

Although many devices like cell phones and PDAs can accept your Address Book contacts, your Personal card is likely to be reduced to "just another card" on those devices when you synchronize. Luckily, Tiger preserves the special status of your Personal card within your Address Book.

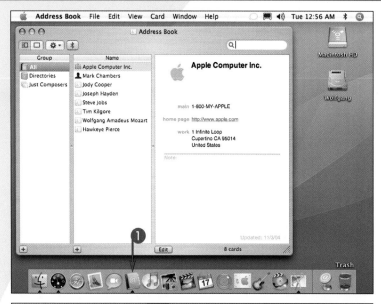

**1** Click the Address Book icon in the Dock.

The Address Book window appears.

**2** Click Card.

**3** Click Go to My Card.

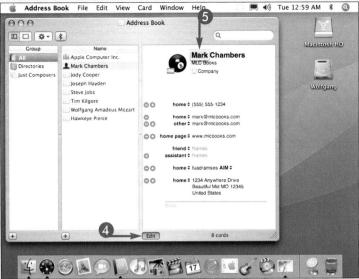

Your personal card appears, denoted by the word *Me* next to the image.

④ Click Edit.

⑤ Click in the fields and edit your personal data.

**# 39**

**DIFFICULTY LEVEL**

⑥ Click Address Book.

⑦ Click Quit Address Book to save your changes and quit Address Book.

## Customize It!

To change the picture that is used on your Address Book card, display your card and drag a new picture from a Finder window to the top of the current picture. If you need to resize the picture, Tiger shows you what the new version will look like; drag the slider to adjust the cropping. When you are satisfied, click Set.

## Customize It!

If you have not selected a card as your Personal card — or if you need to choose another card as My Card — click the desired card in the Name list, click Card, and then click Make This My Card. Address Book assigns the new card as your personal card, and uses that data in other applications.

# ADD A NEW FONT
## to spice up your documents

You can use the Font Book utility application to add new fonts to your system. With Font Book, you can enable and disable specific fonts, making it easier to manage your font collection.

Because Mac OS X can recognize and use both Adobe and Windows TrueType fonts, you have a practically unlimited supply of commercial, freeware, and shareware fonts available — both online and at your local computer software store. Fonts that you add to your system through Font Book are automatically

available for use throughout most of your applications. If you create a document that uses custom fonts, you can export those fonts so that others can install them and open or print the document using a different Macintosh.

With Font Book, you can view samples of every font in your collection, showing each character in the font. Font Book can also display information about each font's format, copyright, and style, which graphic designers and print services use every day.

**1** Click the Finder icon in the Dock.

Tiger opens a new Finder window.

**2** Click Applications in the Finder.

**3** Double-click Font Book.

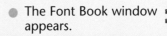
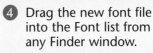

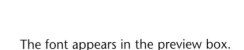

- The Font Book window appears.

④ Drag the new font file into the Font list from any Finder window.

## 40

**DIFFICULTY LEVEL**

The font appears in the preview box.

⑤ Click Font Book.

⑥ Click Quit Font Book to save your changes and quit Font Book.

## TIPS

### Did You Know?

You can create new collections within Font Book that can help organize your fonts according to a theme, family, or type. To do so, click the Add button, which bears a plus sign, and type the name for your new collection. To add fonts, drag and drop them from the Font list to the new collection.

### Did You Know?

You can disable both individual fonts and entire font collections. A disabled font or collection does not appear within your applications or within the Font dialog, which often improves the performance of applications like word processors on older, slower Macintosh computers. You can always launch Font Book again and enable the font or the collection to restore it to active status.

# Working with Multimedia and the Digital Hub

With the return of Steve Jobs to Apple, the Macintosh experience has changed in dramatic ways. Chief among these changes is the arrival of the Macintosh in its role as the "Digital Hub." The idea behind the Digital Hub is that your Mac serves as the centerpiece of your digital world. You can connect still and video cameras, music devices such as the iPod, and CD and DVD burners to your Mac, the Digital Hub. The Mac OS takes care of coordinating tasks between these different devices, interpreting the media that each uses and producing useful output.

To help you along in your pursuit of digital nirvana, Apple saw fit to provide Mac users with iLife '05, a suite of digital media applications that offer professional results with a beginner's learning curve. This suite consists of iTunes and GarageBand for your music, iPhoto for your photographs, iMovie HD for working with video content, and iDVD for creating DVDs that play in home and computer DVD players.

Not only do the Digital Hub applications work great alone, but they also work well together. Apple has gone to great lengths to make the applications interoperate. The result is that your media tasks are easier to perform, take less time, and give you better results. With the Digital Hub, you can combine multimedia from audio, photo, and video sources into professional-looking presentations that you can then burn onto CD and DVD.

# Top 100

# GET PHOTOS
## onto your Mac

You can quickly and easily transfer multimedia from your favorite device. Tiger can transfer and manipulate your favorite image, video, and audio media from digital and video cameras, audio CDs, an iPod, and just about anywhere else you can find it.

You can transfer photographs from digital cameras directly into iPhoto. This gives you the opportunity to tweak the look of the photos, catalog and print them, or even send them to friends. You can also import images into iMovie for use in your own movies.

You can import your favorite video content into iMovie HD. After import, you can add titles, mix in background music, and even add sophisticated professional-quality video effects.

Tiger also includes a complete set of tools for importing and working with audio. You can import your favorite songs from CD and the Internet using iTunes, iMovie HD, and iDVD, or you can create your own original songs with GarageBand. After import, you can catalog and listen to the song in iTunes or mix it in as background music for your movies in iMovie HD and iDVD.

**①** Click the iPhoto icon in the Dock.

The iPhoto window appears.

**②** Connect a digital camera to your Mac.

iPhoto displays the Import window.

**③** Type a new name for this roll.

**④** Type a brief description for this roll.

You can click Delete items from camera to erase the images on the camera after import.

**⑤** Click Import.

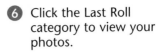

The new images appear in the Last Roll category in the Source list.

**6** Click the Last Roll category to view your photos.

## 41

**DIFFICULTY LEVEL**

**7** Click iPhoto.

**8** Click Quit iPhoto.

## TIPS

### Did You Know?

iPhoto is able to import from a wide range of digital cameras, but not every camera is supported and recognized. If you plug in your camera and iPhoto does not recognize it, make sure that your camera is turned on and ready to upload. To check whether your specific model of digital camera is supported, visit the Support page on Apple's Web site at www.apple.com.

### Caution!

If you choose to erase the images from your digital camera when the import process in iPhoto is complete, be forewarned that you cannot reverse this procedure. After you erase the images from the camera, there is no way to regain them; your only copies of those images are now in your iPhoto library. Use this feature with care!

# BURN CDS AND DVDS
## with iTunes

You can use iTunes to burn your music playlists onto CDs and DVDs in a number of popular formats. The iTunes Preferences window gives you several options for burning discs. You can select the optical drive with which you want to burn, how fast you want the burner to operate, and the format of the resulting burned disc.

You have three format choices for burning discs in iTunes — Audio, MP3, and Data. Audio CDs are the

discs that you will find in your home stereo, computer, boom box, or car. MP3 discs work in some CD players, some DVD players, and nearly all computers, such as your Microsoft Windows brethren. Data discs are only readable with a computer. Note that the Data format enables you to record on a DVD disc as well as a CD; using a DVD is a great way to back up large libraries. Select the appropriate format according to your specific needs.

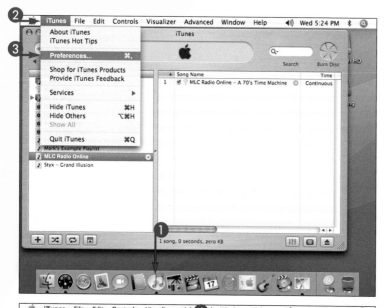

① Click the iTunes icon in the Dock.

② Click iTunes.

③ Click Preferences.

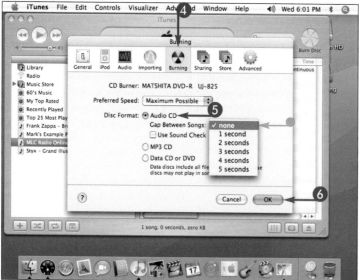

The iTunes Preferences window appears.

④ Click Burning.

⑤ Click the Audio CD option to create an audio CD (○ changes to ◉ ).

● You can click the Gap Between Songs drop-down list and set the amount of silence that you want between each track on the audio CD.

⑥ Click OK.

**7** Click the Add button ( [+] ) to create a new playlist.

**8** Type the playlist name in the Source list.

**9** Drag songs from the library to the playlist.

As you add items, the total time and size of all the files appears here.

**DIFFICULTY LEVEL**

**10** Click the playlist to select it.

**11** Click Burn Disc.

iTunes prompts you to insert a blank disc if one is not inserted already.

**12** Click Burn Disc again.

iTunes begins to record the disc.

**TIPS**

## Apply It!

If you want to burn additional discs identical to one already burned, select the playlist and click Burn Disc again. You can make multiple copies, with one exception: The songs downloaded from the iTunes Music Store have limits on how many copies you can make. The number is large for individual use but is meant to prevent large-scale piracy.

## Caution!

If you use CD-R media, make sure your playlist is set exactly as you want it. If you make a mistake, you waste a CD-R. Although CD-RW discs are erasable and give you more room for error, they cannot make up for the lost time of burning another disc. In addition, older audio CD players cannot read CD-RW discs.

# USE iTUNES AUDIO
## in iMovie HD

You can use audio that you have imported into iTunes with the projects that you create in iMovie HD. This helps you keep audio files organized with iTunes excellent playlist feature while maintaining one-click access to that content in iMovie where you can use it.

You can use audio from iTunes to add background music for romantic movies, sound effects for action clips, and voice-over narration for documentaries. When you add iTunes audio to an iMovie HD project, iMovie HD imports a copy of the audio, which

becomes part of the current iMovie HD project. By importing the audio into your iMovie HD project, you keep the original iTunes audio unaltered for future use.

In iMovie HD, you can preview the audio you imported, adjust its volume, use it in a movie clip, and even fade it in and out. Again, the changes that you make to the audio in an iMovie HD project are saved separately by iMovie HD, so those changes do not affect the original audio in iTunes.

1 Click the iMovie HD icon in the Dock.

2 Click Audio to display the audio tray.

Your iTunes Library and playlists appear in the audio tray.

3 Click a song that you would like to use in a movie from one of your playlists.

4 Drag that song from the audio tray to an audio track in the Timeline.

5 Click here and select iMovie Sound Effects.

6 Drag a sound effect from the audio pane to the second audio track in the Timeline.

If you rewind the movie and click the Play button, iMovie HD mixes the two audio tracks together upon playback.

**7** Drag the sound effect and place it somewhere earlier in the Timeline.

**8** Click the Play button.

iMovie HD instantly remixes the audio tracks, accounting for any changes that you made.

**DIFFICULTY LEVEL**

**9** Click the sound effect that you added to the track.

**10** Press ⌘–C to copy the sound effect to the Clipboard.

**11** Click Edit.

**12** Click Paste.

When you paste the sound effect, iMovie HD creates a copy of the audio snippet in the same track, immediately following the sound effect that you copied. This is handy for duplicating a sound quickly.

**TIPS**

### Customize It!

Not only can you overlap your imported iTunes sounds in two different audio tracks, but you can even do so in the same audio track. If you drag one imported audio clip on top of another audio clip, the two clips will play back mixed together, at approximately the same volume.

### Did You Know?

You can create echo effects by layering multiple copies of the same audio clip. To make the audio echo, move each clip to a position slightly later in the Timeline than its preceding clip. You can also adjust the volume of each clip, with each sound becoming quieter. The clips that form the echo can appear in the same track or in different tracks.

# USE iPHOTO IMAGES
## in iMovie HD

You can take advantage of the organization that iPhoto affords you and maintain one-click access to iPhoto images in iMovie HD, in which you can use the images as part of a movie project.

Using your own images from iPhoto to create title screens, movie credits, background images, or animated photo slideshows is easy. When you add iPhoto images to an iMovie HD project, iMovie HD imports a copy of the photo as a separate still image, which in turn becomes part of the current iMovie HD

project. By importing the images into your iMovie HD project, you keep the original iPhoto images unchanged for other uses.

In iMovie HD, you can zoom in on a still image, place it in the frame wherever you want, add professional-looking animated titles, and apply motion effects to it. The changes that you make to a still image in an iMovie HD project do not affect the original photo in the iPhoto Library.

① Click the iPhoto icon in the Dock.

② Import a photo from a digital camera.

   *Note: See Task #41 for more information.*

   iPhoto adds the photo to the Photo Library.

③ Click the newly imported photo from the Photo Library.

④ Click Edit.

● You can adjust the brightness, contrast, red-eye reduction, and other aspects of the photo.

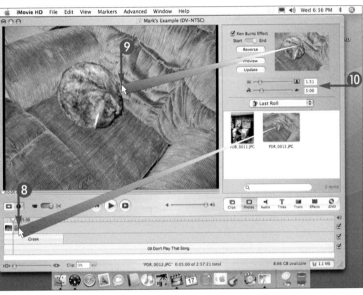

**5** Click the iMovie icon in the Dock.

**6** Click Photos to reveal the photo tray.

Your iPhoto Photo Library and photo albums appear in the Photos pane.

**7** Click a photo that you would like to use in a movie from one of your photo albums.

**8** Drag that photo from the Photo pane to the topmost track in the Timeline.

**9** Drag the Duration and Zoom sliders to adjust your settings.

**10** Click Update to apply the changes that you made to the photo.

# TIPS

## Did You Know?

When you customize an existing image in iPhoto that you imported earlier in iMovie HD, those changes are not reflected in the iMovie HD version of the image; the two images are now stored separately on your hard drive. You must re-import the modified image back into your iMovie HD project for the changes to appear in your movie.

## Caution!

When preparing images for use with iMovie, keep in mind that they should maintain a size ratio of 4 x 3 with 768 x 576 being the minimum dimensions. Using an image that does not conform to a 4 x 3 ratio may result in iMovie HD cropping the image to conform to 4 x 3, with lackluster results. Use a graphics application like Photoshop Elements to resize the image.

# FADE iMOVIE HD AUDIO
## in and out

You can fade iMovie HD audio in and out over time. The iMovie HD interface has a convenient Timeline in which you arrange audio clips in the order that they will play during the movie and adjust the volume of the audio over time.

To create a fade, you first place two markers on the volume level bar in the Timeline. You adjust the volume of the second marker in relation to the first marker, making its volume lower.

Fading is useful for a multitude of tricks. Using two audio tracks — one with music and the other with speech — you can fade music to a lower volume when someone speaks. After the speech is completed, fade the music back in at a higher volume. You can also use fades to create audio effects that were not part of the original clip. As someone walks closer to the camera in a clip, for example, slowly increase the volume of the footsteps in the audio track. You will be surprised how professional the results seem when you use tricks like these.

① Click the iMovie HD icon in the Dock.

② Click the Timeline Viewer button.

The separate tracks appear in the Timeline at the bottom of the iMovie interface.

③ Click Audio.

The audio pane opens.

④ Drag an audio clip from the audio tray to the Timeline Viewer.

⑤ Select the audio clip in the Timeline.

⑥ Click View.

⑦ Click Show Clip Volume Levels.

A horizontal volume-level line appears in the audio clip.

⑧ Click the horizontal line to add a handle to the audio clip.

A small circle appears on the horizontal volume level bar.

⑨ Drag the newly added handle toward the top of the volume-level bar.

The volume increases at that point in the audio clip.

⑩ Click the horizontal line and add another handle to the right side of the previous handle in the audio clip.

⑪ Drag the handle toward the bottom of the volume-level bar.

The volume decreases from the level of the first handle to the level of the second handle, fading the audio out upon playback.

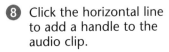

## 45

**DIFFICULTY LEVEL**

---

## TIPS

### Customize It!

You can continue adding volume handles throughout the track to adjust its volume over time, allowing for control that is more precise during each scene. Using this technique, you can make a significant jump or drop in volume for a particularly dramatic effect at the proper point in your movie.

### Did You Know?

To delete a handle, select it and press Delete. If you accidentally delete a handle that you did not want to eliminate, you can get it back: Press ⌘–Z to undo your action. The handle reappears with its curves intact. You can even undo multiple mistakes. If you inadvertently erase three handles, for example, press ⌘–Z three times to reinstate them in the Timeline.

---

# Add or remove the
# KEN BURNS EFFECT

When you work with photographs in iMovie, you can apply the famous "Ken Burns Effect" to an image. This effect adds motion to otherwise lifeless still images. Used sparingly, the Ken Burns Effect helps you create dramatic iMovie HD clips with just a few still images. If you use it too often, however, your movies can take on a gimmicky, if not seasick, feel.

Ken Burns is a world-renowned filmmaker, known particularly for creating documentaries. One of his signature styles is an effect whereby he positions a still photograph in front of a movie camera. He then slowly moves the camera past the image and zooms in or out on the photograph, instilling a unique feel to the photograph when viewed as a movie. You have, no doubt, encountered this effect in many television programs and movies. When you know what it looks like, you will find it popping up everywhere. The Ken Burns Effect simulates this fancy camera work digitally.

Although the Ken Burns Effect can make your photographs fun to watch, remember that a little goes a long way.

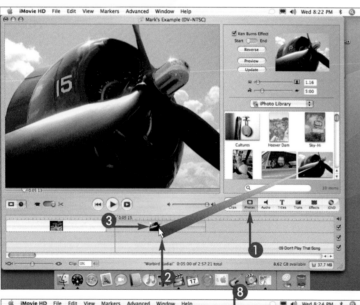

### ADD THE KEN BURNS EFFECT

① Click Photos in iMovie.

The Photos pane appears.

② Drag a photo from the photo pane to the Timeline.

③ Click the new clip in the Timeline to select it.

④ Click the Start option.

⑤ Drag the slider to adjust the speed and scale parameters for the starting image.

⑥ Click the End option.

⑦ Drag the slider to adjust the speed and scale parameters for the end of the clip.

⑧ Click the Ken Burns Effect check box (☐ changes to ☑).

⑨ Click Update to add the effect to your photo clip.

⑩ Click to uncheck the Ken Burns Effect check box (☐ changes to ☑).

⑪ Click Update.

The Ken Burns Effect is removed from the clip.

**DIFFICULTY LEVEL**

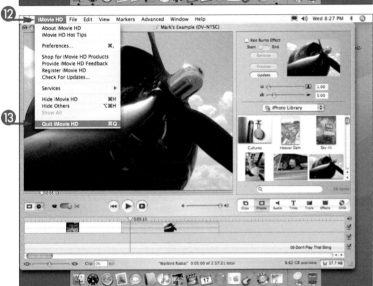

⑫ Click iMovie.

⑬ Click Quit iMovie.

## TIPS

### Apply It!
You do not have to use the Ken Burns Effect only for the standard narrative effect that he uses. For example, you may remember scenes in movies that slowly pan from someone's feet to their head to indicate that they are very large or tall. You can accomplish this feat with the Ken Burns Effect, too.

### Customize It!
You can use the Ken Burns Effect to simulate the frame shaking. Move the image upward a small amount in the Preview window and set the speed for a very quick transition. Add the clip to the Timeline. Repeat the same effect in the reverse direction and add the clip to the Timeline. The quick up and down oscillations produce a believable frame movement.

# EXPORT iMOVIES
## for use in the hub

You can export your completed iMovie HD content to one of several formats: By default, you can export to a video camera, to a QuickTime file, or to an iDVD-ready file. If you have Roxio Toast installed, you may also see a VCD option in the Share dialog.

Video camera sharing sends the completed movie to a connected video camera. You can then use the camera as an intermediary to transfer the movie to a VCR or other similar device.

Sharing to iDVD simply presets the export settings to use the DV format that is appropriate for iDVD and

Apple's DVD Studio Pro. If you need finer control over these settings, you can accomplish the same thing by exporting to QuickTime and making the settings by hand.

QuickTime export gives you the chance to export your movie to a large variety of video formats, including DV, AVI, and MOV.

You can also send your movie through email using Apple Mail, or publish a movie on your .Mac Web site. If you have Bluetooth hardware, you can even save your movie to a remote Bluetooth device!

### OPEN THE SHARE DIALOG

1 In iMovie HD, click File.

2 Click Share.

### EXPORT TO A CAMERA

The Share settings appear.

3 Click the Videocamera tab.

4 Check to make sure that your camera is in VTR mode with a writable tape in it.

5 Click the Share button.

The movie is exported to the camera.

## EXPORT TO iDVD

⑥ Click the iDVD tab.

⑦ Click the Share button.

The movie is exported directly to the iDVD application.

**DIFFICULTY LEVEL**

## EXPORT TO QUICKTIME

⑧ Click the QuickTime tab.

⑨ Click here and select a compression level from the Compress movie for drop-down list.

*Note: For example, you can choose Web or Full Quality DV (Digital Video).*

⑩ Click the Share button to save the movie for the selected format.

## TIPS

### Customize It!

iMovie makes life easier by offering you several preset QuickTime formats. If these formats do not meet your needs, choose Expert Settings from the Compress movie for drop-down list to manually select a QuickTime export format.

### Did You Know?

QuickTime Pro offers many more features for exporting video than the standard version of QuickTime. To register for QuickTime Pro, open the QuickTime pane of System Preferences. Click Registration and enter your registration code. If you do not have a code, click Register Online in the registration window.

### Caution!

Video files are large. In fact, sometimes they are huge. Make sure that you have enough hard drive space before you decide to make several copies of your movie in DV format.

# EXPORT iPHOTO IMAGES
## into iMovie HD

The iPhoto application gives you many different options for exporting photographs to use in other applications. You can export an image or entire rolls of images.

You can use the File Export tab of the Export Photos dialog to save images in JPG, PNG, and TIFF formats. JPG is useful for Web pages, e-mail attachments, and general-purpose uses where smaller file sizes are needed. TIFF files are much larger than JPG, but they also do not suffer from the degradation that JPG files do.

You can export a roll of photographs as a set of Web pages by exporting via the Web Page tab, which offers settings that affect the HTML output of the export. You can upload this export to your Web site or store it on your hard drive for personal use.

The QuickTime tab permits you to save the image or roll as a QuickTime movie. This works well for creating a slideshow movie or when you need the QuickTime format for a still image in another application.

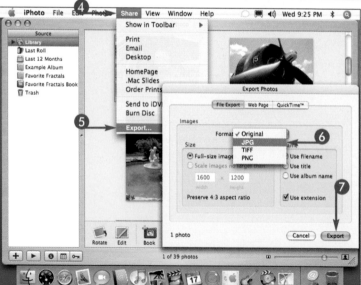

### EXPORT AS A JPEG

1. Click the iPhoto icon in the Dock.

2. Click Library in the Source list.

3. Click the photo that you would like to export from the Library.

4. Click Share.

5. Click Export.

   The Export Photos dialog appears.

6. Click the Format drop-down arrow and select JPG as your image format.

7. Click Export to export the image.

⑨
⑧

⑩

EXPORT TO QUICKTIME

⑧ Click to select a photo album in the Source list.

⑨ Click Share.

⑩ Click Export.

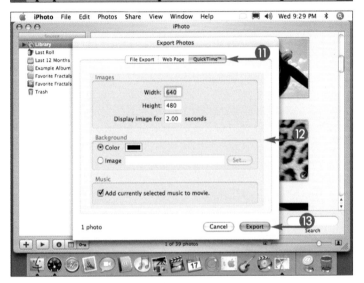
⑪
⑫
⑬

The Export Photos dialog appears.

⑪ Click QuickTime.

⑫ Adjust the settings for your QuickTime movie.

⑬ Click Export.

iPhoto creates a QuickTime slideshow movie from your photo album, including subtle transitions.

**TIPS**

## Customize It!

The images that iPhoto uses do not necessarily have to be photographs. For example, you can create an image in a graphics application such as Adobe Photoshop and import the image into iPhoto. This means that you can create a title page, text annotations, and other images, which you can in turn use as part of a QuickTime export in iPhoto.

## Did You Know?

Besides exporting images from an entire photo album, you can export individual photos to share as well. Click the Library or a specific album in the Source list, then select each of the images that you want to export by ⌘-clicking each one. After you have selected the desired images, export them as shown in this task. iPhoto exports only the selected photos.

# Use iTunes to
# CROP AND SPLIT FILES

If you have an audio file that you would like to crop — that is, remove some of the audio, like cropping a photo — you can use iTunes to perform the operation. Cropping is not the most intuitive operation, but it is simple to use. This is handy when you want to remove extraneous sound at the beginning and end of an audio file. Cropping is also useful for isolating a small snippet of sound from a file.

Using a similar set of operations, you can also separate a lengthy file into smaller chunks, each of which is a new audio file. This is great when you have extremely long audio files that you would like to split. This may happen, for example, when you record an LP record. It is easier to simply record an entire side of an album and then chop it up in iTunes later, rather than start and stop the recording process for each song on the album.

① Click the iTunes icon in the Dock.

② Click a playlist name.

③ In the playlist, click a song from which you would like to copy a segment.

④ Listen to the song and locate the exact times of the clip segment you would like to copy.

*Note: To locate where you would like the clip to start, move the playback head in the display to the desired point. Write down that time. Then move the playback head to determine the end time of the segment.*

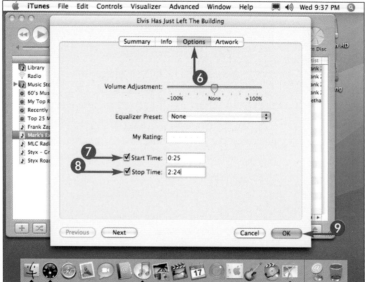

⑤ Press ⌘–I.

The Info window opens.

⑥ Click Options.

⑦ Click Start Time (□ changes to ☑) and type the beginning time of the segment to copy.

⑧ Click Stop Time (□ changes to ☑) and type the ending time of the segment to copy.

⑨ Click OK.

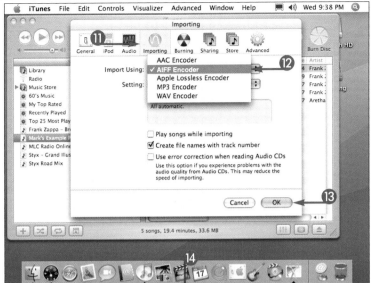

⑩ Press ⌘-, (comma).

The iTunes Preferences dialog appears.

⑪ Click Importing.

⑫ Click the format of the new clip; for example, select AIFF Encoder.

⑬ Click OK to apply the settings and dismiss the Preferences dialog.

⑭ Click Advanced.

⑮ Click Convert Selection to AIFF.

iTunes converts the segment that you defined into a new track.

iTunes plays a "ding" sound when the conversion is complete.

## TIPS

### Did You Know?

When you extract a segment from an audio file in iTunes, iTunes gives the copy the same name as the original. Locate and rename the file as soon as you have finished creating it to ensure you do not delete the wrong file. If you are not sure which file is which, look at the time column of both tracks — the smaller one is the copy.

### Apply It!

After you complete the first conversion, you can continue separating audio segments from the file in a similar fashion. Select the start and end points as before, and perform a new conversion for each segment that you would like to extract. Do not forget to rename the new file each time.

# CONVERT AUDIO FORMATS
## with iTunes

You can convert audio with the import tools built into iTunes — whether you are preparing audio for use on an audio CD or as content for a Web page.

Some audio applications require audio files to be in a particular format — AIFF or WAV. If you have files that are not in these formats and you need to convert the files to AIFF or WAV, you can convert the audio when you import it. (iTunes automatically takes care of all conversions for you when you burn an audio CD.)

You can also import audio with the MP3, Apple Lossless, and AAC formats. These file formats offer good audio content with smaller file sizes than AIFF and WAV. MP3 preceded AAC, so it is more universal. AAC provides a better-sounding file that is smaller than MP3, but you may not notice the difference. Apple Lossless format provides the best sound quality, but the files are significantly larger than AAC or MP3. If you are importing audio for your personal playlists, go with Apple Lossless or AAC.

1 Click the iTunes icon in the Dock.

The iTunes window appears.

2 Click iTunes.

3 Click Preferences.

The Preferences window appears.

4 Click Importing.

5 Click here and select AIFF Encoder from the Import Using drop-down list.

6 Click here and select Custom from the Setting drop-down list.

The AIFF Encoder dialog appears.

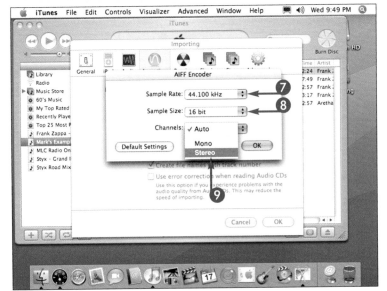

**7** Click here and select 44.100 kHz from the Sample Rate drop-down list.

**8** Click here and select 16 bit from the Sample Size drop-down list.

**DIFFICULTY LEVEL**

**9** Click here and select Stereo from the Channels drop-down list.

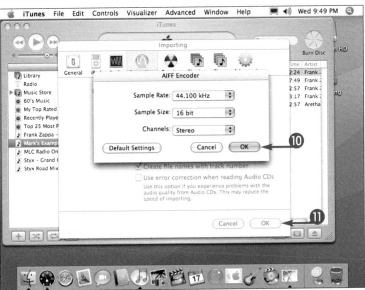

**10** Click OK.

**11** Click OK in the Preferences window.

### Did You Know?

If you are importing new tracks to trade with Windows users — or friends who use other types of MP3 players besides the iPod — then you should definitely select MP3 as your format for importing songs. Your friends are more likely to have a computer that recognizes MP3 than AAC or Apple Lossless, although this gap is narrowing.

### Did You Know?

If you are wondering what sound quality you should select while importing tracks in MP3 format, remember that audio CDs use a 128 kbps sampling rate, so to achieve CD quality you should choose a minimum of Good Quality (128 kbps). If file size is less of an issue, the Higher Quality (192 kbps) setting is preferred.

# 6

# Troubleshooting Problems and Seeking Help

Even if you are the most knowledgeable Mac power user, you will still encounter problems. You will eventually need to determine what is wrong with Mac OS X Tiger before you can fix it. This process is called *troubleshooting,* an acquired skill that takes a little practice and a lot of logical deduction. Luckily, Tiger is very reliable, so you should not have to troubleshoot often. Apple provides you with tools to help you track down both hardware and software tribulations.

But what if you cannot fix what is broken? Believe it or not, even Apple support technicians are stumped from time to time. Therefore, it is important to know where to

turn for help in case you get stuck in the troubleshooting process.

In this chapter, you learn how to troubleshoot problems in Tiger and how to locate additional help resources using Sherlock. These tasks introduce troubleshooting applications included with Tiger — such as the Disk Utility and Activity Monitor — and discuss how you can use them to both monitor your system and fix many hardware and software errors. You will also find a number of Tiger's more common features for dealing with problems such as updating Mac OS X, forcing a misbehaving application to quit, and booting from a CD-ROM.

# Top 100

# FORCE QUIT
## a program

You can terminate a misbehaving program without losing your other open documents, which comes in handy on those rare occasions when an application may freeze or lock up and you cannot use the familiar ⌘-Q shortcut to quit. For example, games are a prime candidate for lockups. A locked-up application may make you nervous — especially if you have important documents open in other applications — but rest easy! Tiger keeps each application that you are running separate in its own area of memory, protected from other applications. If a game crashes or your video-editing application locks up, you can force it to quit.

In the event that a Tiger UNIX system failure occurs — called a *kernel panic* — Mac OS X stops entirely and displays a black rectangle with white text on your screen. If you experience a kernel error, you have to shut down your Mac manually by holding the Power button down for a count of three to four seconds. When you restart your Mac, Tiger may take a bit longer to boot while it checks your hard drive.

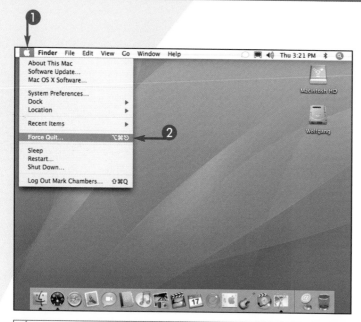

1 Click **.
2 Click Force Quit.

The Force Quit Applications dialog appears.

3 Click the application that you want to quit.

4 Click Force Quit.

Tiger displays a confirmation dialog to make sure that you want to force quit the application.

⑤ Click Force Quit.

Tiger forces the application to quit.

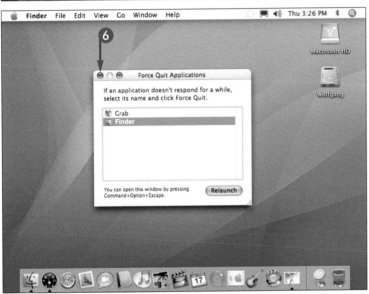

⑥ Click the Close button in the Force Quit Applications dialog.

## Caution!

Forcing an application to quit results in the loss of any changes you have made to the documents that application was using. In addition, the document may not open again due to corruption. Always make sure that an application is definitely locked up instead of just hard at work calculating something before you force it to quit.

## Did You Know?

When an application locks up, you may not be able to see the Apple menu icon; for example, a full-screen application may hide the Finder menu. If this happens and you need to use Force Quit, you can press ⌘–Option–Escape to display the dialog, or you can press ⌘–Tab repeatedly to cycle through your open applications and activate the Finder menu.

# Use Mac OS X
# HELP

You can use Tiger's very extensive online Help system to search for specific keywords that describe a problem you are having or a feature you have not used yet. Many Help topics include links that take you to other relevant Help topics, making it easier to narrow down your search to find the specific information you need. You will also find that a number of topics enable you to open System Preferences panes or launch applications.

Most of the applications within Tiger's Help system have a dedicated top-level menu, which often

includes a list of the features that are new with the latest version, as well as what has changed since the last full version of Mac OS X.

The Help system displays its own window; you can resize the Help window and move it anywhere you like on your desktop. Many Mac users keep the Help window visible while they follow the steps it provides to solve a problem or to try out a new feature inside Tiger.

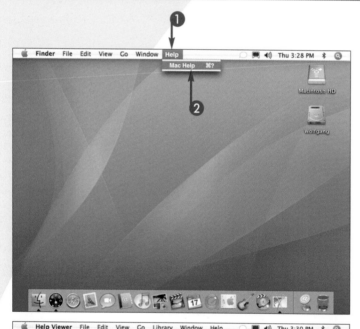

① Click Help on the Finder menu bar.

② Click Mac Help.

The Mac Help Viewer window appears.

③ Click in the Search box.

④ Type the word that you want to search for and press Return.

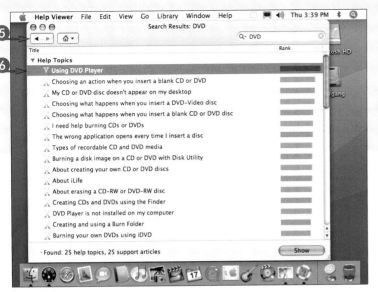

Mac OS X displays the Help topics that contain (or reference) your keyword.

⑤ Click the arrows to move backwards or forwards through the topics you have viewed.

⑥ Double-click a topic to open the topic in the Help Viewer.

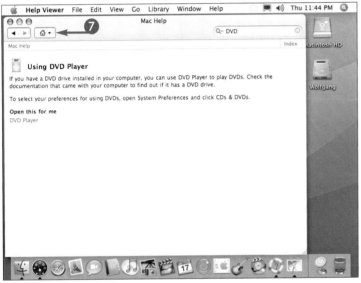

⑦ Click the Home button to return to the top-level Help page.

⑧ When you have finished searching the Help system, press ⌘–Q to exit the Help Viewer.

## Did You Know?

Third-party applications can add their own Help topics to the Apple Help Viewer list; so, as you install additional applications over time, you may find yourself locating more Help information than you expected. To check for Help material specific to the application, just search for the application name. Other commercial applications, like Microsoft Office 2004, may actually have their own Help system.

## Did You Know?

For an overview of the most important new features in Tiger, click What's New in Tiger? within the Help Viewer. If you have never used Mac OS X before, click New to Mac OS X? to display tips and procedures for those switching to Tiger from Mac OS 9 or Windows XP.

# Fix hard drive problems with the
# DISK UTILITY

You can use Tiger's Disk Utility application to fix hard drive errors and faulty permissions on your system. Hard drive errors can be caused by any number of events: a power loss, a misbehaving application, or physical damage caused by extreme heat or vibration. Disk Utility can repair many types of errors that may crop up in your hard drive's folders and files. Of course, it cannot fix a hard drive that has been physically damaged, but then again, no software utility can! In case of physical damage to your hard drive, you will have to replace the drive and restore your data from your backup.

There are a number of third-party commercial disk utilities that perform much the same diagnostic and repair functions as Tiger's Disk Utility. However, two applications — Drive 10 from Micromat at www.micromat.com, and Norton Utilities at www.symantec.com — can both defragment your hard drive. Defragmenting can significantly improve the performance of your hard drive, so these utility applications make good additions to the Disk Utility, which does not defragment your drive.

**①** Press ⌘–N.

A Finder window appears.

**②** Navigate to the Utilities folder, which is inside the Applications folder.

**③** Double-click Disk Utility.

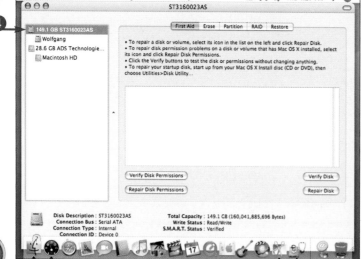

The Disk Utility window appears.

**④** Click the hard drive that you want to verify or repair.

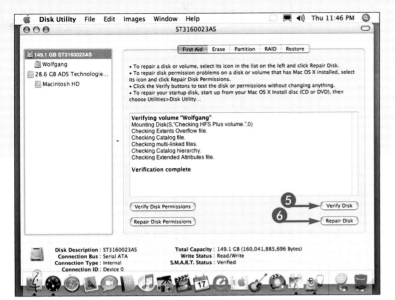

The Disk Utility displays the statistics for the partition and some buttons.

5 If the Verify Disk button is enabled, you can click it to verify the file structure of the drive.

The Disk Utility displays the result of the disk verification.

6 If a problem is found with your disk format, click Repair Disk to fix it.

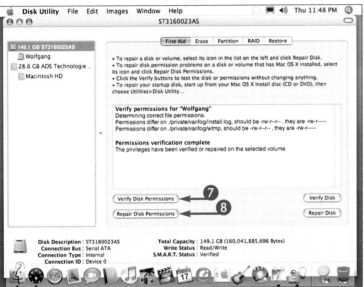

7 To verify the drive's file permissions, click Verify Disk Permissions.

The Disk Utility displays the result of the permissions verification.

8 If a problem is found with your drive's disk permissions, click Repair Disk Permissions to fix it.

9 Press ⌘–Q to exit the Disk Utility and return to the Tiger desktop.

## Did You Know?

Mac OS X Tiger automatically and invisibly runs the Disk Utility, verifying and repairing the boot hard drive when you turn on your Macintosh. This helps keep your drive running smoothly behind the scenes. Tiger also performs a limited defragmenting process each time you access or open a file. It still helps, however, to perform a full defragmentation with a commercial utility.

## Did You Know?

You cannot verify or repair files on your boot drive because Tiger is currently using it. However, if you are having problems starting your Mac and Tiger will not complete the boot process, you can force Tiger to boot from the DVD. Load your Mac OS X installation DVD and shut down your Mac and then turn it on while holding down the C key.

# MONITOR
## your Mac's
# PERFORMANCE

When troubleshooting Tiger or a Macintosh application, it is often helpful to monitor how much memory, processor time, and system resources are being used. Tiger provides the Activity Monitor, a utility program that displays these figures, along with network and hard drive usage, in real time. You can also display a number of different real-time indicators that will remain on your desktop for as long as Activity Monitor is running. These indicators help you monitor your Mac's processor activity.

The Activity Monitor also enables you to view the processes being executed by Tiger. A *process* is a discrete task, either visible or invisible, that Tiger performs in order to run your applications or to keep itself running. For example, the Dock and Finder are actually processes, as are Microsoft Word and Photoshop. You can select a process and click Inspect on the Activity Monitor toolbar to display more information on that process, or force a process to quit to troubleshoot a problem.

**1** Press ⌘–N.

A Finder window appears.

**2** Navigate to the Utilities folder, which is inside the Applications folder.

**3** Double-click Activity Monitor.

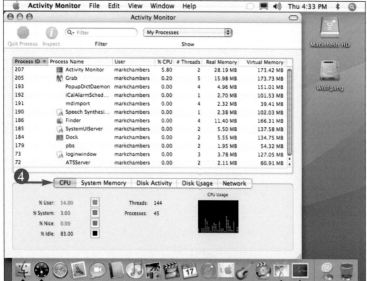

The Activity Monitor window appears.

**4** Click the type of information that you want.

*Note: The Activity Monitor can display CPU usage, memory usage, disk activity and usage, and network activity.*

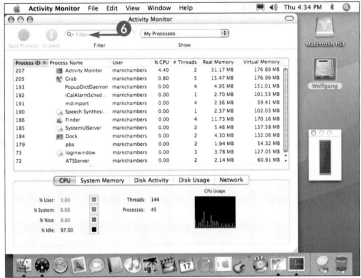

⑤ Press ⌘–2 to display a separate CPU Usage window.

You can move this window anywhere on your desktop and monitor your CPU usage.

⑥ Click the Filter box and type a text string.

Activity Monitor displays only the process names containing the text.

⑦ Click Activity Monitor.

⑧ Click Quit Activity Monitor.

# TIPS

## Caution!

Using the Activity Monitor, you can selectively quit a process, just as you would force an application to quit, as shown in Task #51. However, deleting a system process (such as the kernel task) can result in all of Mac OS X locking up! It is a good idea to delete a process only if instructed to do so by a support technician.

## Did You Know?

You can click View→Dock Icon to access a submenu with different types of Activity Monitor information; for example, you can choose to monitor your disk activity, CPU usage, or network usage. When you select one of the submenu items, Activity Monitor displays that information as an animated Dock icon, updated in real time, so that you can hide the Activity Monitor window.

# Search the AppleCare
# KNOWLEDGE BASE

You can use Sherlock's AppleCare Knowledge Base section to search for solutions to problems or step-by-step procedures to make configuration changes to your system. Although you may already consider Sherlock helpful in researching all sorts of things on the Internet — from the spelling of a word or the show times for a movie to flight schedules, stock quotes, and driving directions — Tiger power users know that Sherlock is also the perfect sleuth for delving into the Apple's comprehensive AppleCare Knowledge Base. You will need an active Internet connection to use Sherlock because it searches the Knowledge Base online.

The AppleCare Knowledge Base provides you with the latest help from Apple technical support, including solutions and workarounds to help you deal with specific third-party hardware and commercial application software under Mac OS X. The results that Sherlock returns are sorted with the most relevant topics displayed first, so you can locate the information you are interested in as quickly as possible.

① Press ⌘–N.

A Finder window appears.

② Navigate to the Applications folder.

③ Double-click Sherlock.

The Sherlock window appears.

④ Click AppleCare.

The AppleCare pane appears.

⑤ Type a keyword, topic, or part of an error message into the Topic or Description box.

⑥ Click the magnifying glass button.

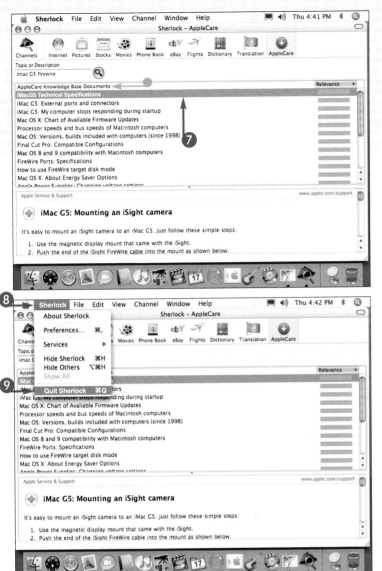

Sherlock displays the Knowledge Base topics that match your target phrase, grouped according to likely relevance.

● You can click AppleCare Knowledge Base Documents to sort alphabetically.

⑦ Click a topic.

Sherlock displays the topic's contents.

Drag the handle on the horizontal divider to make the topic pane larger.

⑧ Click Sherlock.

⑨ Click Quit Sherlock.

## Did You Know?

AppleCare and Sherlock make a great team, especially when you are searching for additional help with the text from an error or warning dialog. Choose the phrase from the error message that is most likely to return a match. If you are having problems with a specific application, do not forget to run a separate search using just the application name.

## Did You Know?

It is a good idea to limit your search text to four words or less, which will return more matches than a longer phrase. Whenever possible, use a phrase from the error or warning message you received, like *DVD eject problem* or *Dashboard widget folder*. Because the results are arranged according to relevance, the answer to your question may appear close to the top of the list.

# UPDATE
## Mac OS X

You can use Tiger's Software Update feature to download and apply the latest operating system updates and patches — either manually, or on an automated daily, weekly, or monthly schedule. Mac OS X may be both remarkably powerful and stable, but there is no such thing as the perfect operating system. Therefore, Apple has added an easy-to-use update system that you can use to install the latest bug fixes, operating system improvements, and Apple application updates.

You can download updates in the background, so that Software Update does not appear until there are actual system files or applications to update. Alternately, you can choose what updates you want to apply, which can save you downloading time if you do not need a particular update.

Unfortunately, you cannot use Tiger's update feature without an Internet connection; and the update process requires much more time if you are using a dial-up modem instead of a broadband (cable modem or DSL) connection.

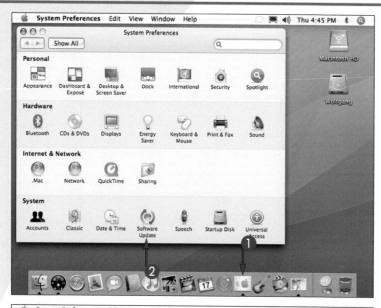

① Click the System Preferences icon in the Dock.

The System Preferences dialog appears.

② Click Software Update.

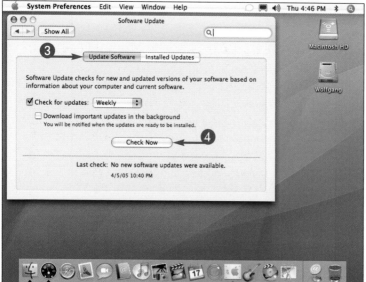

The Software Update pane appears.

③ Click Update Software.

④ Click Check Now to manually check for updates.

*Note: Some updates require that you restart your Mac and will prompt you for permission to do so.*

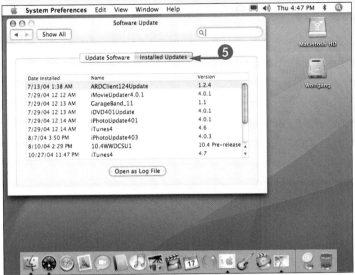

**5** Click Installed Updates to display software updates you have already installed.

**# 56**

DIFFICULTY LEVEL

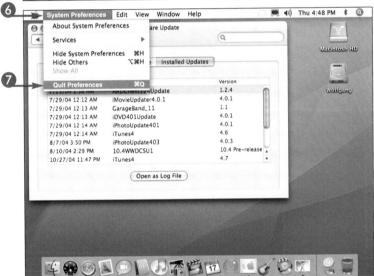

**6** Click System Preferences (if you did not have to restart).

**7** Click Quit Preferences.

## TIPS

### Customize It!

You can set Tiger to automatically check for updates behind the scenes: click the Check for Updates check box to enable it, and then click the time period drop-down menu to specify the schedule. If you want Mac OS X to automatically download critical updates as well, click the check box labeled "Download important updates in the background" to enable it.

### Did You Know?

If any updates appear, it is usually a good idea to install all of them — even those updates that do not apply to your current system. For example, you can always apply any AirPort updates to Mac OS X, even though you do not currently have an AirPort Extreme network card. If you do add wireless networking to your Mac in the future, Tiger will be up-to-date.

# BOOT
## from a
# CD-ROM

You can force Tiger to boot from your Mac's optical drive to help troubleshoot or repair your computer. What should you do if Tiger itself locks up during the boot process? It is hard to troubleshoot Mac OS X if the operating system constantly freezes because of a system or hard drive error. Luckily, you are not limited to booting from your Mac's internal hard drive. You can also boot Tiger from an external hard drive. Alternately, in a pinch you can actually boot Tiger from your Mac OS X installation CD-ROM or DVD-ROM.

This trick also comes in handy when you want to boot from a third-party utility CD-ROM or DVD-ROM, such as Norton Utilities from Symantec (www.symantec.com) or TechTool Pro from Micromat (www.micromat.com). These utility applications typically include a bootable version of Mac OS X on their installation discs, enabling you to boot Tiger and then run the utility — all from a single CD-ROM or DVD-ROM!

1 Load the disc from which you want to boot.

2 Verify that the disc icon appears on the desktop (if possible).

3 Click .

4 Click Restart.

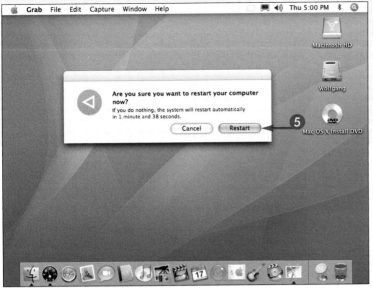

The Restart confirmation dialog appears.

⑤ Click Restart.

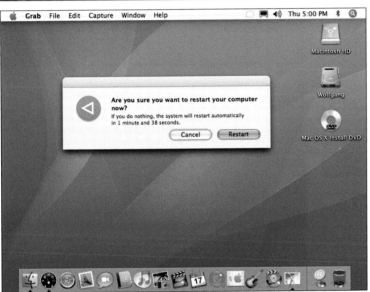

⑥ Press and hold the C key on your keyboard.

Your Mac boots from the disc.

## TIPS

### Did You Know?

You can eject a CD-ROM or DVD-ROM even if Mac OS X does not finish the boot process. Restart Tiger by turning your Mac off and back on again, if necessary and hold down the mouse button, or press the Media Eject key if your Mac has one as soon as you hear the startup chord.

### Did You Know?

To display a graphical system boot menu during startup, which acts much like the Startup Disk pane in System Preferences, hold down the Option key while starting or restarting your Mac. This boot menu enables you to select an external hard drive, CD-ROM, or DVD-ROM as your boot drive, rather than your Mac's internal hard drive.

# UNINSTALL APPLICATIONS
## the correct way

You can uninstall applications that you no longer use and save space on your hard drive. Unlike Windows, Mac OS X does not include an Add/Remove Applications utility; most Macintosh developers follow the rule "One folder for each application." All the data files, and the application program itself, reside in a single folder, and usually all you need to do is delete that folder to uninstall the application.

There are exceptions, so follow the steps shown here each time you delete a Mac OS X application folder. Search for any Preference or data files that remain in

other locations and delete them to save space on your hard drive and keep things neat!

An application preference or data file that is left behind after the main application has been deleted is commonly called an *orphan*. The more applications you install and subsequently remove, the more likely your hard drive contains orphan files that are simply taking up space.

1. Press ⌘–N.

   A Finder window appears.

2. Navigate to the folder of the application that you want to uninstall.

3. Control–click the folder and select Move to Trash.

4. Click in the Search box.

5. Type the name of the application that you just deleted.

   **Note:** *For example, you may type* **Photoshop** *or* **BBEdit**.

   Tiger displays all files that include the target word.

**6** Click the disclosure arrow to expand each category.

**7** Click a file.

Tiger displays the path to the file.

**DIFFICULTY LEVEL**

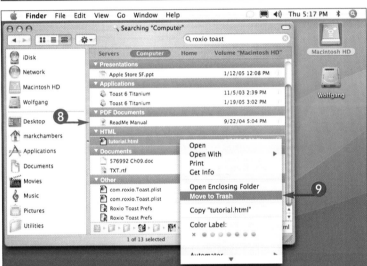

**8** If the file needs to be deleted, Control–click it.

**9** Click Move to Trash from the drop-down menu.

The file is removed from your system.

**10** Repeat steps **7** to **9** for all the files with matching names and version numbers.

**TIPS**

## Did You Know?

There are a number of shareware and commercial utilities that can also perform the uninstall job for you; the best known of the lot is probably Spring Cleaning from Aladdin Systems (www.aladdinsystems. com), which also removes Internet browser cache files and fixes broken aliases. The application even includes a Restore feature that can restore files that you have deleted by accident.

## Did You Know?

Generally, it is safe to delete an orphan file if it shares the same name and version number as the deleted application; however, do not empty the Trash until you have used your Mac for a day without encountering any problems. If you deleted a file that you need, click the Trash icon in the Dock and drag the file back to its original location.

# Fix problems with
# USER ACCOUNTS

If more than one person uses your Macintosh — either from the local keyboard or across a network — you have turned your computer into a multiuser powerhouse. Mac OS X does a great job of keeping your personal documents secure and even maintains different desktop and application settings for each user that you create. Everyone else's documents are kept separate and secure as well because each user has his or her own Home folder. A classroom Macintosh is a good example of a shared multiuser computer: each student has an account, and the teacher uses the Admin account — the primary account created when you first set up Mac OS X.

However, if a person suddenly cannot log in or you have to tweak the capabilities of a user, you need to go troubleshooting in System Preferences; you can use the settings found on the Accounts pane. Note that this procedure assumes that you are logging in as the Admin account.

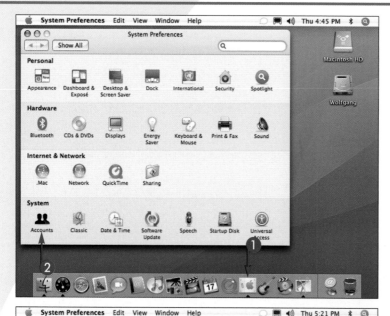

**ACCESS ACCOUNT INFORMATION**

① Click the System Preferences icon in the Dock.

The System Preferences dialog appears.

② Click Accounts.

The Accounts pane appears.

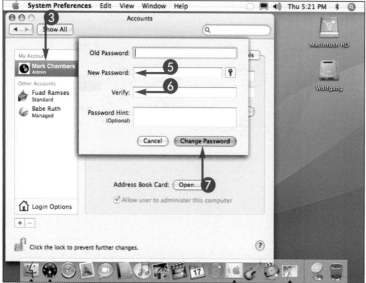

**CHANGE PASSWORDS**

③ Click the user account that you want to configure.

Tiger displays the settings for that account.

*Note: If the user's password is not working, you can reset it here.*

④ Click Change Password.

*Note: Depending on your access level, you may be required to type your old password.*

⑤ Click in the New Password field and type a new password.

⑥ Click in the Verify field and retype the same password.

⑦ Click Change Password.

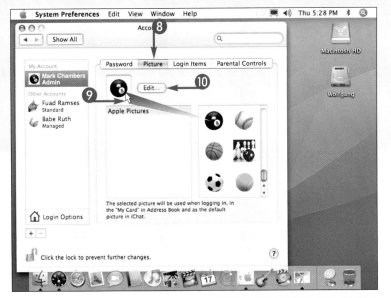

⑧ Click Picture.

The image shown represents the selected user on the login screen.

⑨ Drag an image thumbnail from the right column to the well.

⑩ Click Edit to add your own image.

*Note: You can use a snapshot from your Mac's video camera or drag an image from a Finder window.*

# #59

**DIFFICULTY LEVEL**

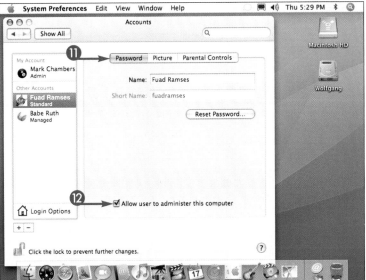

**CHANGE A USER'S PRIVILEGES**

⑪ Click Password.

⑫ Click Allow user to administer this computer to change the account security level (☐ changes to ☑).

*Note: With this check box enabled, the selected user receives all Admin privileges.*

⑬ Press ⌘–Q to quit System Preferences.

## Caution!

A user with an Admin account can make changes within System Preferences, and also has greater access to documents and applications within Tiger. For example, an Admin user can make changes to your network, security, and sharing settings! Therefore, assign Admin privileges only to those who require higher access or experienced Mac OS X users that you trust.

## Customize It!

If you will be the only one using your Macintosh, you can set it to automatically log you in. Click the Login Options button and then click the Automatically Log in As check box to enable it. Choose your account from the drop-down menu. Deleting any old user accounts that you no longer need is always a good idea.

# Rebuild the
# CLASSIC MODE DESKTOP

You can help keep Tiger's Classic environment problem-free by rebuilding your Classic desktop. When you need to run an older application written before the days of Mac OS X, Tiger automatically starts a special environment, called *Classic mode,* in which the application can run smoothly. In fact, the legacy application has no idea that it is actually running in Mac OS X, and you can continue to run your Mac OS X applications right alongside your Classic applications.

Like Mac OS 9 before it, however, your Classic mode desktop may sometimes require a desktop database

rebuild; this can solve a number of problems in Classic mode, including icons that no longer appear on the desktop, and application document icons that no longer display correctly. The desktop database file may be corrupted by all sorts of events, including blackouts, programs that lock up, and running out of hard drive space.

Note that the latest Macintosh computers no longer ship with Mac OS 9. Therefore, you may not need to perform this procedure: it is only necessary if you use Classic mode.

① Click the System Preferences icon in the Dock.

The System Preferences dialog appears.

② Click Classic.

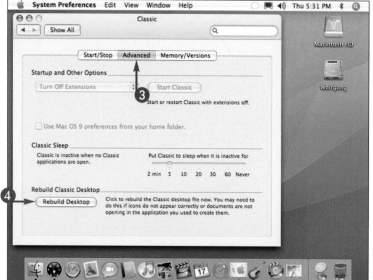

The Classic pane appears.

③ Click Advanced.

④ Click Rebuild Desktop.

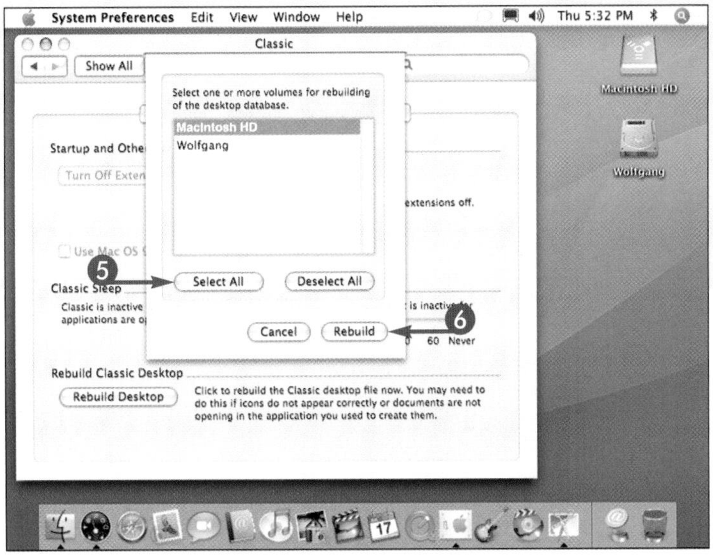


# #60

DIFFICULTY LEVEL

Tiger displays the Volume Selection sheet.

5. Click Select All.

   ***Note:*** *Choosing Select All rebuilds the Classic desktop database using all the volume information from all the drives on your Mac.*

6. Click Rebuild.

   The Classic desktop database is rebuilt.

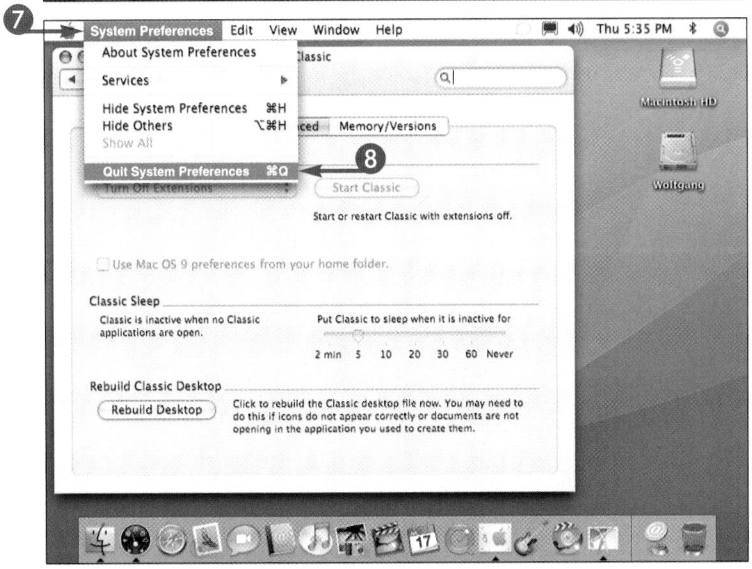


7. Click System Preferences.
8. Click Quit System Preferences.

## TIPS

### Did You Know?

You can configure Classic to run automatically when you log in using the current account. Click the Start/Stop button and check Start Classic When You Log In. To completely hide the Classic launch progress bar, check Hide Classic While Starting. Note, however, that your Mac will run significantly slower every time you boot the computer until Classic mode finishes starting up.

### Customize It!

If you have multiple installations of Mac OS 9, remember that Tiger enables you to choose which Mac OS 9 System folder is used to launch Classic mode. Click the Start/Stop button and then click the System folder that you want to use. By default, Tiger uses the System folder on the same drive as your Mac OS X System folder.

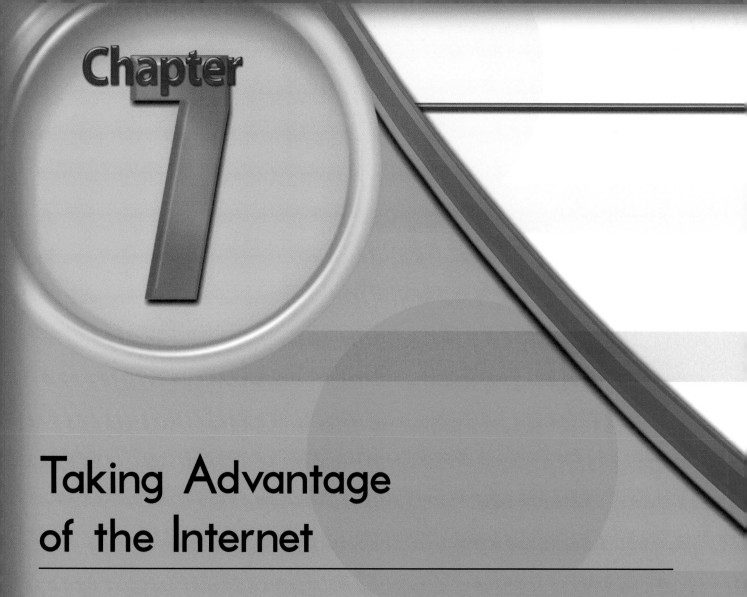

# Chapter 7

# Taking Advantage of the Internet

The Internet has become a major part of the personal computer landscape. Mac OS X has always provided great features to help you work on the Internet. Tiger continues this tradition by updating some existing tools as well as adding new ones to the mix.

Safari, the Web browser included with Tiger, just keeps getting better. With improvements in Safari, you can save entire Web pages to your hard drive, or block unwanted pop-up windows and JavaScript applets.

The Mail application includes antispam features and tight integration with other applications such as the Address Book. Using Spotlight, you can search through all of your e-mail messages in the blink of an eye.

Browsers and e-mail clients are not the only way to use the Internet in Tiger. Sherlock is a great tool for finding specific information on the Web. With Sherlock, you can find what you need in a fraction of the time required using other methods, including searching for phone numbers, reading movie listings, and even tracking eBay auctions.

In addition to browsing the Web, Tiger makes it easy to run your own Apache Web server. With only one click, you can begin serving Web pages on the Internet like the pros. With the power of Apache behind you, you will find that running a Web server also has many benefits on your local network.

# Top 100

# ORGANIZE YOUR WEB SURFING
## with tabs

You can organize and speed up your Web surfing while reducing clutter by using tabs in the Safari Web browser. Tabs enable you to open multiple Web sites within the same browser window and switch between them easily. This prevents you from having to open multiple windows to accommodate multiple Web sites.

After you activate tabbed browsing in Safari, you can use tabs much as you would use the Open in New Window menu command in any other Web browser.

Each tab can display its own Web page. You can also open links in new tabs by using the tab keyboard shortcuts.

Each tab, like each window in nontabbed browsers, displays the title of the Web page within it. A tab also lets you know when it has completed the download of the Web page associated with it. Then, when you are finished reading the Web page shown within a tab, you can close it by clicking the tab's Close icon.

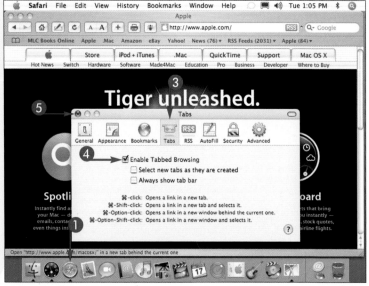

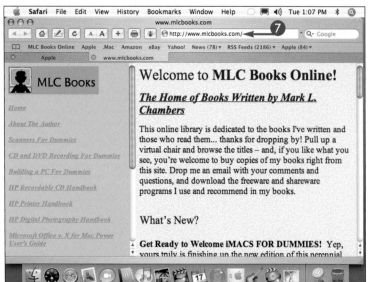

ACTIVATE TABBED BROWSING

① Click the Safari icon in the Dock.

② Press ⌘–, (comma).

The Safari Preferences window opens.

③ Click Tabs to open its settings pane.

④ Click Enable Tabbed Browsing (☐ changes to ☑).

⑤ Click the Close button to close the Preferences window.

Tabbed browsing is now enabled.

⑥ Press ⌘–T.

A new tab appears in the Web browser.

⑦ Type the URL of another Web site and press Return.

*Note: You can also click a bookmark in your Bookmark bar.*

The Web site loads in the new tab.

136

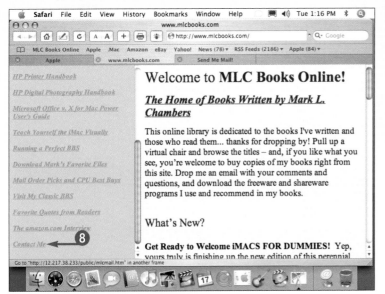

⑧ While pressing and holding ⌘, click a Web page link.

The Web site loads in a new tab, but remains in the background.

⑨ Press ⌘–W to close the current tab.

The current tab closes, and the last tab you opened becomes the active tab.

⑩ Click the Close icon on any tab to close it.

---

**TIPS**

### Did You Know?

You can quickly close all the tabs in a Safari window by pressing ⌘–Option–W. All the tabs you have created immediately close, leaving the enclosing window active. You can also press ⌘–Shift–Left Arrow to open the tab to the left of the current tab, and ⌘–Shift–Right Arrow to open the tab to the right of the current tab.

### Customize It!

By Control–clicking a tab (or right-clicking it if you have a two- or three-button mouse), you can access a few hidden tab features. The contextual menu that appears when you click permits you to open a new tab, or reload or close an existing tab. It also lets you close all other tabs besides the current one.

# SAVE IMAGES AND MOVIES
## for later use

You can save the images and movies you see on Web sites while you are surfing. You may sometimes run into an image that you want to save for later use — perhaps a cool image displayed on a Web site that you want to use for your own desktop or a movie trailer that you want to show a family member who is not at home.

All content that appears on a Web page is actually a file that resides somewhere on your hard drive. The

browser downloaded it to your computer so that you could view it. This means that all the content you see on Web pages is also available for you to use later.

With Safari, you can save images and movies using a number of different methods, such as downloading, copying, saving, and dragging files. None of these is a big surprise for proficient Mac users, but they may not all occur to you.

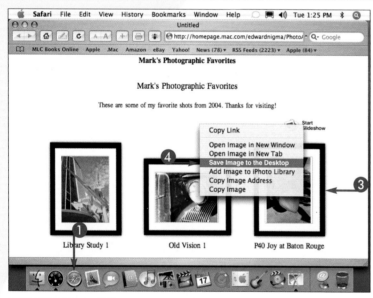

### DOWNLOAD AN IMAGE

❶ Click the Safari icon in the Dock.

❷ Load a Web page containing an image that you want to save.

❸ Control–click the image.

A contextual menu appears.

❹ Click Save Image to the Desktop.

Safari downloads the image and saves it to your desktop.

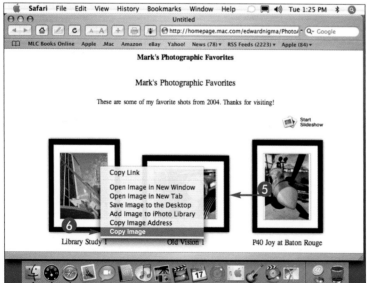

### COPY AN IMAGE

❺ Control–click the image.

A contextual menu appears.

❻ Click Copy Image.

*Note: You can paste the image from the Clipboard into most applications, such as AppleWorks, Microsoft Word, or Adobe Photoshop.*

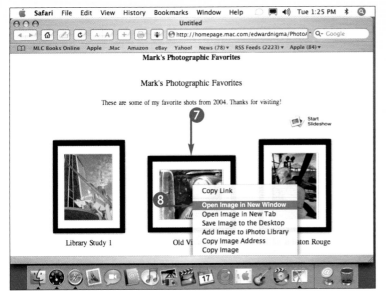

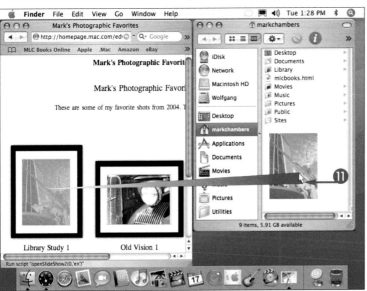

## SAVE AN IMAGE WITH SAVE AS

⑦ Control–click the image.

A contextual menu appears.

⑧ Click Open Image in New Window.

A new window opens with the image in it.

⑨ Press ⌘–S to save the file on your hard drive.

**DIFFICULTY LEVEL**

## DRAG AN IMAGE TO THE FINDER

⑩ Load a Web page with an image that you want to save.

⑪ Drag the image directly from the Web page to the Finder.

The image file appears in the Finder.

## Apply It!

To save QuickTime movies in Safari, click the triangle icon in the movie controller and choose Save As Source from the menu. The standard Save As dialog appears, enabling you to save the movie on your hard drive. This does not work for all QuickTime movies because some content is protected by the author. In those instances, the Save As Source menu is dimmed.

## Apply It!

After you copy an image to the Clipboard in Safari, open the Preview application. Click File→New from Pasteboard to create a new image from the Clipboard. You can then export the image to one of a dozen different formats for use in other applications. Remember, however, to honor the creator's copyright.

# Use Sherlock to
# FIND INFORMATION
## and perform tasks

You can put Sherlock to work, locating information like movie schedules and dictionary entries. The Internet is a great tool, but sometimes it is not so good at giving you specific information quickly. Searching for the simplest information can sometimes feel like an exercise in futility. To help you out, Apple created Sherlock. Sherlock attempts to harness some of the more common Internet tasks, presents them in a convenient format, and expedites your search for information.

Whereas the Internet tends to think globally, Sherlock narrows your search and may be best described as acting locally. Sherlock excels at tasks such as finding schedules for your local movie theater, looking up phone numbers for the pizza place down the street, or looking up the meaning of a word.

Sherlock comes with a number of useful utilities, but it can do so much more. Sherlock uses a plug-in format that permits third-party users to extend the functionality of Sherlock. This has led to a proliferation of Sherlock plug-ins that help you do everything from troubleshooting your Macintosh to shopping online.

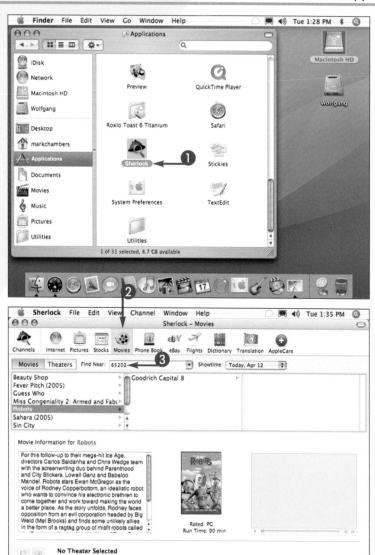

### FIND MOVIES

① Open the Applications folder and double-click the Sherlock icon.

   The main Sherlock window appears.

② Click Movies.

   The Movies interface opens.

③ Type the name of a city or a zip code to find movies playing near your home.

④ Press Return to see the results.

   Sherlock scours the Internet for you and finds the names of all movies playing in your area. It also displays the times and locations where you can see them.

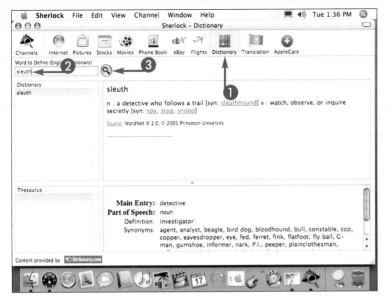

## LOOK UP WORDS IN THE DICTIONARY

1 Click the Dictionary button.

The Dictionary interface opens.

2 Type a word that you would like to look up.

3 Click the Search button.

Sherlock looks the word up for you and gives you the full definition.

# 63

**DIFFICULTY LEVEL**

## ADD A CHANNEL

1 To add a channel plug-in, simply click the link on the Web site where the channel plug-in is located.

2 Click Proceed.

The channel plug-in self-installs in Sherlock.

*Note: The iCalShare (www.icalshare.com) We Speak Sherlock channel is shown here.*

## Apply It!

Many useful Sherlock plug-ins are available on the Internet. You will find plug-ins for searching commercial, government, and Mac-related sites. You can track packages, find sheet music, and read tutorials. Sherlock can do it all. For examples, check out the Web site Sherlock Plug-ins for Power Users (http://pwrsearchr.users1.50megs.com/sherlock/pg1.html). This Web site makes a good jumping-off point for downloading other plug-ins.

## Customize It!

After Sherlock installs a new channel plug-in, you can instantly use it by clicking its icon in the Sherlock toolbar, or you can move your new Sherlock channel icon to another spot in the toolbar before you use it for the first time. Press and hold ⌘ while you drag the icon to its new location in the toolbar.

# Channel the power of the
# ADDRESS BOOK IN MAIL

You can access your Address Book contacts within Mail to make it easier to address your messages. The Address Book application in Tiger is a central repository for all your contact information. It stores names, addresses, telephone numbers, e-mail addresses, iChat and AIM instant messaging addresses, and many other bits of information. The Address Book does a good job of helping you organize all of this information, but this is only part of its true power. The Address Book can also play nicely with the rest of Tiger and the applications on your Mac. Rather than have this type of data stored

multiple times in different applications, it makes sense to store it once in the Address Book. From there, the other applications can access the information automatically and include that information in your documents. Many different applications already support the Address Book protocol.

For example, the Address Book works in conjunction with the Mail application. If you enter e-mail addresses for your various contacts in the Address Book, you can use them in Mail to send e-mails.

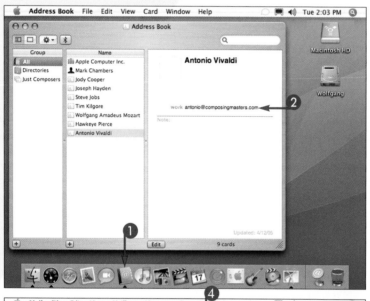

① Click the Address Book icon in the Dock.

② Add an entry for a friend, making sure to complete the e-mail field.

③ Click the Mail icon in the Dock.

④ Click New.

A new blank e-mail message appears.

**5** Click the Address Book.

The e-mail addresses of your friends appear in the Addresses window.

# 64

DIFFICULTY LEVEL

**6** Drag a name from the Addresses window to the To: or Cc: fields of the e-mail message.

The e-mail address instantly appears in the field.

*Note: You can continue dragging and dropping other names to the To: and Cc: fields if you need to e-mail more than one person at a time.*

TIPS

## Customize It!

To export an address from the Addresses window in Mail, ⌘–click (or right-click if your mouse has a second button) on the person's name whom you would like to export. Choose the Export Vcard item from the contextual menu to save the address as a file. You can attach this Vcard file to send e-mail addresses from your Address Book to others.

## Did You Know?

As you use the addresses in Mail, you can continue to make changes to Address Book: just leave the Address Book application window open and minimized, and then click on the minimized window in the Dock to edit a contact. When you switch back to Mail, its address list reflects the changes that you made in the Address Book.

# View and bookmark
# DOCUMENTS IN SAFARI

You can use Safari as a handy means of organizing and viewing documents. Because so many people use Safari as a Web browser, it is no wonder that they often overlook the fact that Safari is also great for other daily tasks. In fact, Tiger power users often leave Safari running, either minimized or hidden, because of its usefulness.

Got an image on your hard drive that you want to view or print? Safari can display it for you, and you can print directly from the Safari window.

Have a movie that you would like to watch? Safari can play it, too.

What makes Safari such a great choice as a document viewer is not just that it can display content. It also has great bookmarking features that you can use to organize your content just as you do Web links. Plus, Safari runs faster and uses far less system resources than a full-featured image-editing application like Photoshop or Corel Painter.

① Click the Safari icon in the Dock.

② Click File.

③ Click Open File.

④ Click a JPEG, GIF, PICT, or PNG image to select it.

⑤ Click Open.

The image appears in a Safari window.

*Note: Besides using the File menu, you can also drag an image file from the Finder and drop it in the Safari window or Dock icon to view it.*

**6** Click Bookmarks.

**7** Click Add Bookmark.

Safari prompts you for a name and location for the bookmark.

**DIFFICULTY LEVEL**

**8** Type a name.

Alternately, you can use the name that Tiger automatically generates.

**9** Click Add.

*Note: You can select the bookmark later by clicking the Show All Bookmarks button to view the content.*

## Customize It!

If you have countless software manuals in Acrobat PDF format on your hard drive, Safari makes it a snap to keep that important information at your fingertips. Create a bookmark for each of your manuals and organize them in the Bookmarks window. Without buying any additional software, you can have a complete library of documentation manuals at your disposal.

## Caution!

Keep in mind that Safari only displays the bookmarked content at a later date if the content stays in the same place on your hard drive. This is a good reason to organize your files according to the Mac OS X standard document file structure using your Pictures, Documents, and Movies folders.

# SAVE WEB PAGES
## on your hard drive

You can use Safari to save Web pages on your hard drive in two different formats. One of the biggest pains about saving Web pages is that they are usually composed of different files like photos and banners. Other browsers force you to save each individual part of the page, which requires knowledge of HTML and the page's source code. Depending on how the Web page is served, this manual method may not even work!

Tiger offers two far more simplified methods of saving Web pages. First, Safari enables you to save

an entire Web page (and all of its associated links) to your hard drive as a Web archive. You can also print the page to a PDF document, maintaining the formatting, images, and fonts. The PDF file looks exactly like the Web page as viewed in the browser.

By using one of these methods, you can make sure that your favorite Web page can be displayed at any time in the future — even if you do not have an Internet connection.

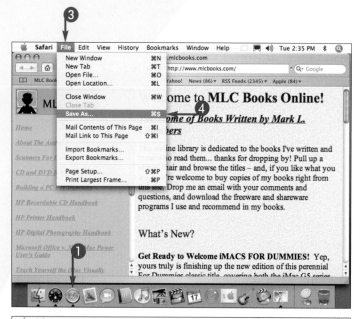

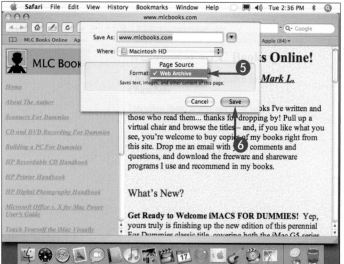

**SAVING A PAGE AS AN ARCHIVE**

① Click the Safari icon in the Dock.

② Load the desired Web page.

③ Click File.

④ Click Save As.

The Save As sheet appears.

⑤ Click the Format drop-down list and click Web Archive.

You can change the file name and location of where to save the archive or accept the defaults.

⑥ Click Save.

Tiger saves the Web page as a Web archive.

SAVING A PAGE AS A PDF FILE

① Click the Safari icon in the Dock.

② Load the desired Web page.

③ Click File.

④ Click Print.

The Print dialog box appears.

⑤ Click PDF to open the standard Save dialog.

You can change the file name and location where to save the page or accept the defaults.

⑥ Click Save.

Tiger saves the Web page as a PDF file.

### Did You Know?

To view the page later, you can double-click it in the Finder to launch Preview, which is a great tool for PDF viewing. Although Preview can display and act on links in PDF files, Tiger's Save As PDF feature does not preserve links. Therefore, if you click a link in your new PDF file within Preview, the link does not work.

### Did You Know?

If you need more features than Tiger's Preview application offers for viewing PDF files, Adobe has a free application called Adobe Reader that you can install on your Mac. Adobe Reader includes a number of functions not included with Preview. For more information on PDF files and a link to the Adobe Reader download Web page, visit www.adobe.com.

# Set up a
# WEB SERVER

You can use the Apache Web server application that comes built-in with Tiger to set up a Web site of your own. Apache is a very popular UNIX Web server application that many individuals and companies around the world use to build and maintain Web sites. Apache is a fully featured Web server, both powerful and reliable, that is easy to use in Tiger. In fact, Apache is already set up in Tiger with the most common default configuration, so you really do not have to install anything. One click is all it takes to start serving Web pages.

After you get your Web server running, all you have to do is add Web pages, and you are ready to roll. By default, there is a Web page installed for the machine as well as one for each user.

Remember, you will need an "always-on" connection to the Internet in order to use Apache as a public web server. For most Mac owners, this means a high-speed DSL or cable modem broadband connection.

① Click the System Preferences icon in the Dock.

The System Preferences window opens.

② Click Sharing.

The Sharing Preferences pane opens.

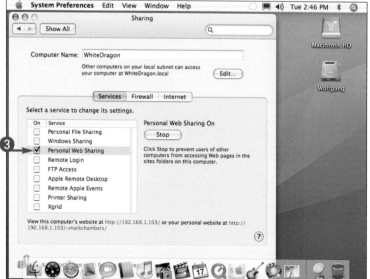

③ Click Personal Web Sharing (☐ changes to ☑ ).

The Apache Web server launches, and you are ready to serve Web pages.

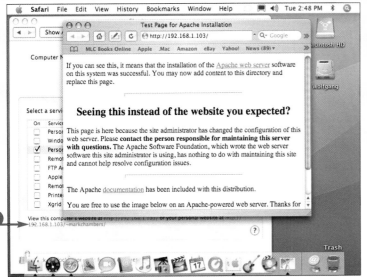

④ Click the View this computer's website link in the Sharing Preferences pane.

Apache displays the default Web page.

⑤ Click the Close button to close the System Preferences window.

## TIPS

### Did You Know?
You can replace the default page with one of your design or edit the existing file. All machines on the local network will be able to access pages on your Web server without any additional work. For computers outside your local network, you will have to open a port on your firewall to permit the accessing of Web pages on your server.

### Customize It!
For a complete guide to configuring and customizing Tiger's Apache Web server, click the Documentation link on the default Web page; this opens the Apache manual in a Safari window. For now, however, you only need to remember that you should store the Web pages you build for your site in the Sites folder, which is inside your Home folder.

# VISIT WEB SITES
## of people in your Address Book

You can easily jump directly to the personal or company Web sites listed for each contact in your Address Book. This saves you the trouble of creating a separate bookmark in Safari for each one of these Web sites.

The Address Book application in Tiger, as you may have guessed, is a utility for storing the contact information for your family, friends, and associates. In addition to names and addresses, you can also store e-mail addresses, personal and business

telephone numbers, iChat and AIM addresses, notes, and Web home pages for each contact you create in your Address Book.

The Address Book is tightly integrated with many applications in Mac OS X Tiger, including the Safari Web browser and Tiger's Mail application. You can view URLs that you enter into your Address Book using Safari, or add the e-mail information stored in your Address Book to the addresses of new messages you compose in Mail.

1. Click the Address Book icon in the Dock.

2. Click the Add button to create a new entry.

3. Type the required information, making sure to complete the home page field.

4. Click the Edit button to save the entry.

5. Click the Safari button in the Dock.

6. Click the Bookmarks button.

The Bookmarks page appears.

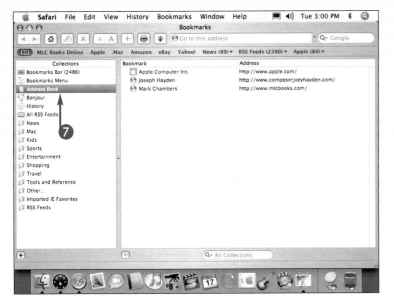

**DIFFICULTY LEVEL**

⑦ Click the Address Book in the Collections pane.

The home pages appear in the View pane.

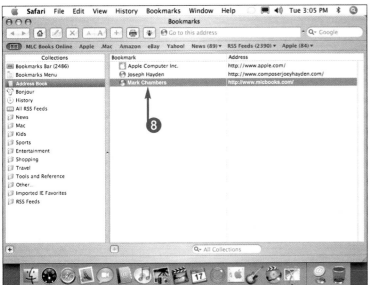

⑧ Double-click one of your friend's home pages to load it in the browser.

**TIPS**

### Customize It!

You can drag addresses from the Address Book section in Safari's Bookmarks page to other bookmark folders. This is handy for organizing your various friends' and contacts' home pages with other Web pages that may pertain to them. You can also drag home page entries from the Address Book section to the Finder to create a URL file.

### Did You Know?

URLs can be added to the right side of the Dock, enabling you to launch Safari and load a page with one click. Drag a home page entry from the Address Book section of the Bookmarks page to the right side of the Dock. This only works if the URL is positioned to the right of the thin vertical line in the Dock.

# ELIMINATE SPAM
## with Mail

You can use the Junk Mail feature in Apple's Mail application to screen and eliminate spam from your e-mail Inbox. Spam is one of those things that people love to hate, and not without reason. Insidious junk mail has taken over many people's mailboxes with ridiculous offers and scams, wasting hours of valuable time. Many computer users maintain a second e-mail address for use on Web sites, in order to deflect spam from their primary address. Some junk mail messages even arrive with malicious viruses and Trojan horse programs as

attachments. Fortunately, the Mail application that ships with Tiger has some great utilities that help tame the beast that is spam.

Perhaps the biggest nuisance of spam is the fact that it is not always easy to determine which e-mail is spam and which is not. Through an ingenious use of color-coding, Mail makes it easy to identify spam with only a quick glance. Plus, you can quickly indicate to Mail that a message is not spam and deserves to be in your Inbox, or visa versa.

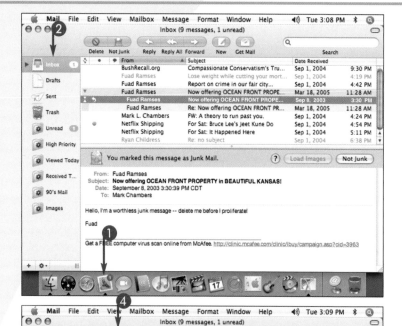

**1** Click the Mail icon in the Dock.

The Mail window appears.

**2** Click the Inbox within the Mailbox panel.

If the Mailbox panel is hidden, press ⌘–Shift–M.

Messages that Mail thinks are spam appear in a tan color in your Inbox list.

**3** Click a message entry that is not marked as spam.

**4** If a message is actually spam, click the Junk icon in the toolbar.

The message is automatically marked with the tan color in your In mailbox list.

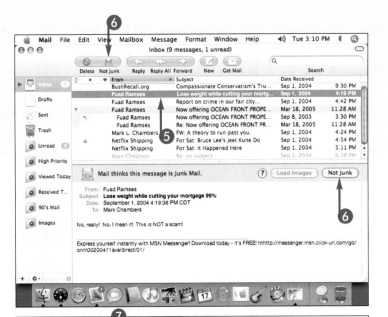

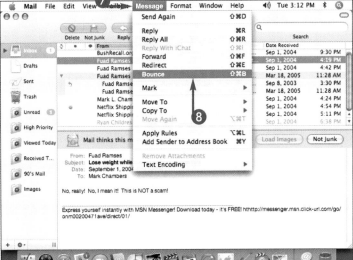

**DIFFICULTY LEVEL**

⑤ Click a message entry that is marked as spam.

⑥ If the message is actually not spam, click Not Junk in the toolbar or the message header.

⑦ To reject a junk mail message, click Message.

⑧ Click Bounce.

Bounced messages are returned to the sender, so it appears that your e-mail address is invalid.

### Customize It!

If you do not like the brownish shade that Mail uses to mark spam e-mail, you are free to change it. Click Mail→ Preferences. In the Preferences window that appears, click the Rules button. In the Rules list, select the Junk item and click the Edit button. Change the color to one that is more to your liking.

### Did You Know?

As you let Mail know which messages are spam and which are not, it learns to identify spam better as time progresses. When Mail is catching nearly all spam messages correctly, you can click Mail→Preferences and click Junk Mail to switch to Automatic mode. A separate Junk mailbox appears and junk mail no longer shows up in your Inbox.

# Stop bombarding
# POP-UP ADS AND
# JAVASCRIPT APPLETS

As the Web has grown, businesses have found it harder and harder to grab your attention. To keep your eyes focused on their products, businesses have resorted to all sorts of tricks. Some of these include dirty tricks such as pop-up windows or hidden JavaScript applets. Without you knowingly taking an action, advertisers like to display a window, usually a smaller size than most Web pages, that contains a small ad. After you surf through a couple of Web pages with this feature, it feels like you are being

bombarded with advertisements splattered over every page. JavaScript applets can even attempt to install programs, both good and bad, on your Mac.

Safari has some great features to help you avoid this hassle: the Block Pop-Up Windows and Disable JavaScript options. With the right settings, you can block those pesky pop-up windows from ever appearing, and prevent a Web site from performing hidden actions on your computer using JavaScript.

① Click the Safari icon in the Dock.

The Safari window appears.

② Type in a Web address for a page with pop-up ads and press Return.

③ Click Safari.

④ Click Block Pop-Up Windows to enable it.

⑤ Press ⌘–R to reload the page.

The ad does not appear.

⑥ Click Safari.

⑦ Click Preferences.

⑧ Click the Security button.

⑨ Click the Enable JavaScript check box to disable it (☐ changes to ☑).

⑩ Click the Close button to close the Preferences dialog.

## Customize It!

While you are checking out the Security pane of the Preferences dialog box, you can also choose not to accept *cookies,* small files saved to your hard drive that help a Web server identify you. In general, cookies are fairly innocuous; but you can choose never to accept them, or to accept them only from sites you choose to visit.

## Did You Know?

Disabling pop-up windows may prevent you from taking certain actions on a specific Web page, for example, an online store may display your shopping cart in a pop-up window. If a feature on a Web site does not appear to work, try enabling pop-up windows while you are on that page by toggling the pop-up protection on and off with the ⌘–K key sequence.

Chapter 7: Taking Advantage of the Internet    155

# Chapter 8

# Making the Most of Your Network Connection

Ever since the Internet boom of the 1990s, it seems that everyone and everything is networked. Mac OS X Tiger keeps pace with all the latest networking developments. With Tiger, you can use the network to share files with Macintosh and Microsoft Windows computers as well as devices like the iPod.

File sharing is just one of the many uses of a network connection available to you in Tiger. Using iChat, you can trade files, exchange text messages, and even teleconference with full motion video and high-quality audio. With iTunes, your can turn your network into a jukebox instantly. Using practically any application, you can send faxes to anywhere in the world.

Besides communication and multimedia, the network is great for utility purposes. Using the Terminal application, you can remotely control other computers on the network, repair a frozen Mac, and even peek at hidden files on an iPod. Tiger supports all sorts of networking protocols and even has a built-in software firewall.

Printing is yet another perfect use for your network. With a few simple clicks, you can share printers on the network. This gives multiple computers on the network the option of printing with the same printer.

# Top 100

# SHARE MUSIC
## over your network with iTunes

You can turn your Mac into a high-tech jukebox without doing much work at all, using iTunes and your wired or wireless network. iTunes is already a sort of jukebox for your personal music, but iTunes also has a great sharing feature that lets you listen to the music in your iTunes library on any Mac on your network that has a copy of iTunes installed.

After you activate music sharing within iTunes, you can listen to music that is located on other Macs on

your network. Likewise, other Macs can view and select individual songs or playlists from your library. The Source list of the iTunes interface lists the shared tunes and even displays the other users' playlists. You can elect to share your entire music library, or specify which playlists in your library are to be shared with others. If security is an issue on your network, iTunes also offers password protection for your shared music.

ACTIVATE SHARING

1. Click the iTunes icon in the Dock.

   The iTunes window appears.

2. Click iTunes.

3. Click Preferences.

4. Click Sharing.

   The Sharing pane of the Preferences window appears.

5. Click Look for shared music (☐ changes to ☑ ).

6. Click Share my music (☐ changes to ☑ ).

7. Click OK.

**#71**

**PLAY MUSIC ON YOUR NETWORK**

⑧ Launch iTunes on a PC or Mac on your network.

The iTunes window appears.

⑨ Click a shared music server on your local network in the Source list.

**Note:** *Shared music servers appear with a blue icon representing multiple pages.*

⑩ Click the song that you would like to hear.

⑪ Click the Play button.

The song begins to play.

## TIPS

### Customize It!

Because iTunes shares your playlists, you might consider other possible uses for them. For example, you can make a playlist customized for each member of your family or your co-workers at the office. Further, by activating and deactivating playlists in the Sharing pane of the iTunes Preferences window, you can restrict which elements of your library that you want to share.

### Caution!

If you are running a software firewall application on your PC, you may have to configure it to allow your music to be shared over your network. This is not a problem if you're sharing music with iTunes on a Mac running Tiger, because Mac OS X automatically updates your built-in firewall configuration within System Preferences when you enable music sharing.

# Audio and video conferencing
# WITH iCHAT

You can use iChat to talk to your friends, family, and co-workers; it works across both your local network and across the Internet. Connect a microphone and a camera to have your iChat buddies see and hear you. Most current Macintosh models (both desktop and notebook) have built-in microphones; many cameras, such as Apple's iSight, have built-in microphones as well. If you do not have a camera but you do have a microphone, you can chat with audio only. If your

buddies have neither a camera nor a microphone, they can still see and hear you, even if you cannot see and hear them.

iChat can use data taken from your Address Book contacts to automatically add those people to your iChat Buddy list. If the person is not in your Address Book yet, iChat will prompt you to enter the person's AIM screen name or his or her Mac.com account name.

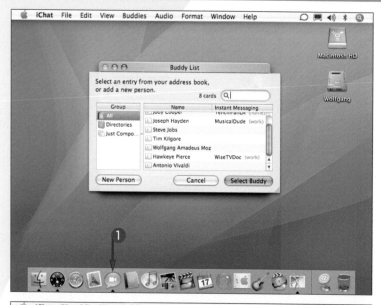

### ADDING A BUDDY FROM YOUR ADDRESS BOOK

**①** Click the iChat button in the Dock.

iChat launches.

**②** Press ⌘-Shift-A.

The Address Book sheet appears.

**③** Click the name of the person you want to add.

**④** Click Select Buddy.

MAKING THE AV CONNECTION

⑤ Click View.

⑥ Click Show Audio Status to toggle it on.

**Note:** *AV-capable machines on the network have small camera and audio icons next to the buddy name.*

⑦ Click a buddy with audio capability in the Buddy List.

⑧ Click the Start an Audio Chat button.

## TIPS

### Did You Know?

The iChat application is compatible with AOL Instant Messenger and uses its network for communication, but it can also function on its own without the AOL network. Using iChat, you can connect and talk to people on your local network without ever logging in to AOL's network. Tiger automatically adds anyone using iChat to your local network list, which appears in a separate window.

### Did You Know?

The latest version of iChat enables you to hold audio-only conferences with up to 10 buddies, all with full-duplex sound (meaning that participants can speak and listen at the same time). iChat can include up to three other buddies in a full video chat. You can display a visual volume cue that makes it easy to tell who's talking at the moment.

# SHARE MUSIC
## on a network drive

You can mount a shared volume from another Mac or PC computer on your network to share your digital music files. After you have the volume mounted, it acts like any other folder on your machine. Add music to your iTunes Library as you normally would, but use the networked folder instead.

The benefit of this method versus the automatic sharing in iTunes is flexibility. By sharing music on a shared volume, you can add items on the remote

computer to your own playlists. You can also edit information about a song, such as its title and artist.

To begin playing music, choose the song that you want to hear and click the Play button. You can even use an old computer as a music server on your Ethernet network. Even though the old Mac may not support the latest version of OS X, if it can support an HFS+ drive (Mac OS 8 and later), you can use it with your slick Tiger machine.

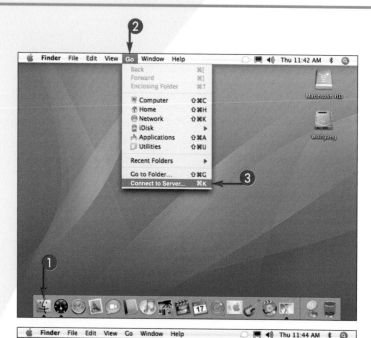

1. Click the Finder icon in the Dock.
2. Click Go.
3. Click Connect to Server.

The Connect To Server dialog appears.

4. Type an IP address.

Alternatively, you can click Browse to locate a server on the network.

5. Click Connect.

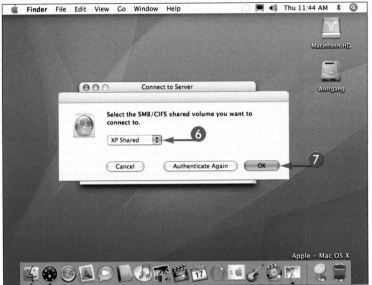

**6** Click the volume drop-down list box to choose a shared volume from the server.

**7** Click OK.

DIFFICULTY LEVEL

**8** Double-click the shared volume on your desktop to open it.

**9** Drag the music files from the remote folder to iTunes to add them to the library.

## Caution!

Although it is technically possible to burn a CD using files over the network, you cannot always guarantee that a network is going to transfer fast enough. Therefore, it is a good idea to copy files from remote computers to your Mac before trying to burn them to a CD. By using local files, you can accelerate the burning process.

## Did You Know?

Sharing music with another computer across your network is fun, but sharing music with two computers is twice as fun. As your music collection grows and your available hard drive space decreases, you can store all sorts of music files on other computers on the network. Remember, iTunes is free for Windows users as well!

# REMOTELY CONTROL COMPUTERS
## on your network

You can remotely control other computers on the network in much the same way as your own. Using the command-line application Terminal and the command-line program `ssh`, you can remotely launch applications, work with files, and even shut down computers without walking into another room.

Before you get started controlling a remote computer, you need to activate remote access for it. You will also need to make sure that you have an account on the remote machine; you can create a new account for yourself if necessary. If you're setting up remote

control on a business network, ask the system administrator for permission first.

Back on your own computer, launch the Terminal application. Now you are ready to control the remote machine with `ssh`, a command-line program you run from Terminal.

When you connect to a remote computer, you cannot use the mouse to control the remote machine, but you can use any installed command-line program. For example, you can launch iTunes by typing only two lines of text in Terminal.

① On the remote computer, click the System Preferences icon in the Dock.

The System Preferences window opens.

② Click Sharing.

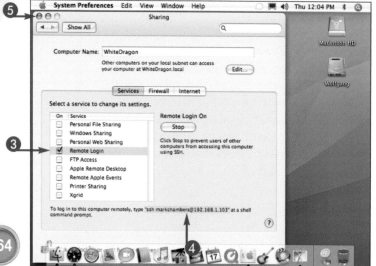

The Sharing pane of System Preferences appears.

③ Click Remote Login (☐ changes to ☑).

④ Write down the `ssh` command as shown in the Sharing pane.

⑤ Click the Close button in the System Preferences window.

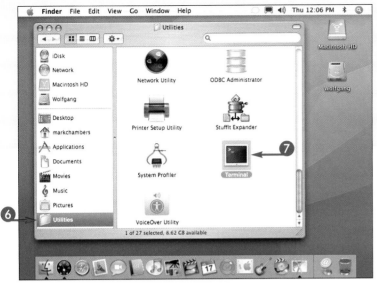

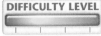

⑥ In a Finder window on the local computer, click Utilities.

⑦ Double-click Terminal.

The Terminal application launches.

**DIFFICULTY LEVEL**

⑧ Type the `ssh` command you wrote down in step **4** and press Return.

⑨ When prompted, enter your account password on the remote computer and press Return.

⑩ Type **cd /Applications** and press Return.

⑪ Type **open iTunes.app** and press Return to launch iTunes on the remote machine.

### Caution!

The `ssh` tool is extremely powerful. A hacker using `ssh` to access your Mac can cause considerable problems for you. Create accounts in System Preferences only for trustworthy people. You should also restrict administrative accounts to those whom you especially trust. It is a common security principle that a safe machine is a disconnected machine.

### Did You Know?

Whenever you are not using remote login, it is a good idea to deactivate it in the Sharing pane of System Preferences. Hackers cannot connect via `ssh` if you have this turned off. The same holds true for all items in the Sharing pane: If you are not using a service, turn it off. Your machine will run faster as well.

# SHARE FILES
## with Windows computers

You can use Tiger to readily share files with both Macintosh and Microsoft Windows computers. Through the technology named Samba, Macs no longer have any problems talking to their Microsoft Windows brethren. Tiger uses Samba behind the scenes to communicate with Windows computers, which makes them appear much like a Mac on the network.

You can activate Windows file sharing in the Sharing pane of System Preferences and then view shared

Windows files in the Finder. Any files or folders that you have shared on your Windows system will appear in a Finder window if you click the Browse button. Otherwise, you are free to connect directly to the Windows machine by means of its IP address.

After the shared folder icon appears on your desktop, you can open it as you would any folder. You can copy files from the shared Windows folder to your local hard drive, or open them as shared documents.

① Click the Finder icon in the Dock.

② Click Go.

③ Click Connect to Server.

A network dialog appears, enabling you to connect to your servers.

④ Click Browse.

A Finder window appears, showing you the available computers on the network to which you can connect.

⑤ Double-click the Windows workgroup folder containing the desired server.

The computers with shared files, or servers, appear.

**6** Double-click a server to connect to it.

# 75

**DIFFICULTY LEVEL**

**7** Click the volume drop-down list box to choose a shared volume from the server.

**8** Click OK.

The shared folder appears on your desktop.

## TIPS

### Did You Know?

You can turn on file sharing for a particular folder in Windows by right-clicking its icon. From the pop-up menu that appears, choose Sharing and Security. In the window that appears, you can activate sharing for the folder as well as assign a network name for the folder, which you'll see in the drop-down list box in step **6**.

### Customize It!

To allow servers and shared folders to appear on your Tiger desktop, you must first change your Finder preferences. Click Finder and click Preferences, and then click the General button in the toolbar. Click the Connected servers check box to enable it. With this feature turned on, Tiger automatically adds an icon for a server on your desktop as soon as you connect.

# SHARE PRINTERS
## with other computers

You can share printers on your network. This enables you to use one printer with multiple computers. Because printers are devices that you probably do not use continuously, it makes sense to share them with other users on the network. Sharing printers can save you time and money. You do not have to invest extra money in multiple printers, and you get more work done because you are not always running into another room to print on another computer.

You can activate printer sharing in the Sharing pane of System Preferences. If you activate Windows

sharing, even Microsoft Windows computers can print to shared Mac printers.

When printer sharing is activated, other users on your home or office network can access shared printers by using the standard Print dialog. Tiger supports a wide array of printers, but only if you install their drivers. The Tiger installation disks contain numerous print drivers for you to use, and your printer manufacturer should also supply you with print drivers for your specific model.

① Click the System Preferences icon in the Dock.

The System Preferences window opens.

② Click Print & Fax.

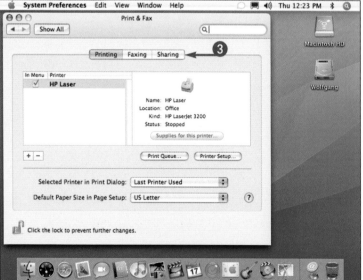

The Print & Fax pane of System Preferences appears.

③ Click Sharing.

168

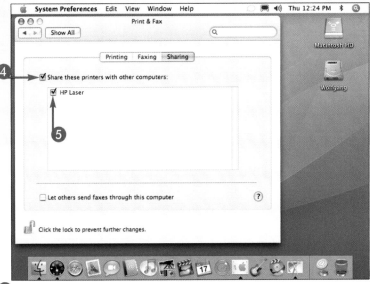

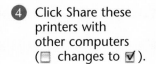

④ Click Share these printers with other computers (☐ changes to ☑).

Printer sharing is activated.

⑤ Click the check box next to each computer that you want to share (☐ changes to ☑).

# 76

**DIFFICULTY LEVEL**

⑥ Click System Preferences.

⑦ Click Quit System Preferences.

## TIPS

### Customize It!

To print a document from another Mac on your network to your shared printer, you must pick your shared printer within the Print dialog. From within any application, press the ⌘-P keyboard shortcut to display the Print dialog, and then select your shared printer from the Printer pop-up menu. Click Print, and your printed document is sent to your shared printer!

### Caution!

If you make a mistake and print the wrong document, click the Printer Status icon in the Dock. In the Printer Status window, you can cancel jobs or deactivate printing altogether. If the printer has a technical problem, you will also find alerts about the problem in the Printer Status window. The alerts help you diagnose and repair the problem.

# Unfreeze a
# FROZEN MAC
## over the network

You can force a frozen or unresponsive application to quit by clicking the Apple menu and choosing Force Quit; from the Force Quit dialog, click the offending application and click Force Quit. However, sometimes even the Force Quit command will not "thaw" a frozen Mac. Even with the power of UNIX behind them, computers can still sometimes act up. Using the Terminal application via another computer on the network, though, you can log in to the offending machine and manually stop whatever is freezing your Mac.

The easiest way to remotely connect to another Mac on a network is to use a tool called ssh. It enables you to connect to another machine and issue it commands as if you were actually sitting in front of the machine. The ssh tool operates in a secure fashion, so you can be reasonably certain that other users on the network will not be able to "watch" your activities as you work.

① Click the Finder icon in the Dock on a Mac on your network that isn't frozen.

② Click Utilities.

③ Double-click Terminal.

The Terminal application launches.

④ Type **ssh –l username ipaddress**, and press Return.

*Username* is your account on the frozen computer and *address* is the IP address of the frozen computer.

⑤ Type your password and press Return.

⑥ Type **top** to see what processes are currently running on the remote machine.

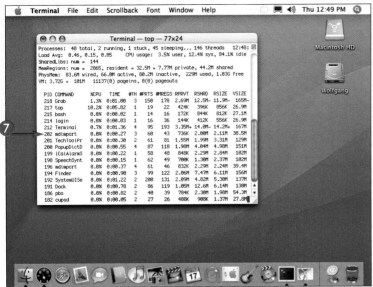

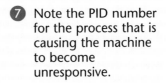

**DIFFICULTY LEVEL**

⑦ Note the PID number for the process that is causing the machine to become unresponsive.

*Note: You can often tell which process is the culprit by looking at the CPU column. If one of the numbers seems especially large, that may be the offending process.*

⑧ Press Control-C to stop the top program.

⑨ Type **kill pidnumber**, replacing *pidnumber* with the PID number of the frozen application.

⑩ Press Return.

The process that you chose is forced to quit. If you correctly chose the offending process, the unresponsive machine becomes responsive again.

**TIPS**

## Put It Together!

Before you can unfreeze a Macintosh over your local network, you must first activate Remote Login in the Sharing pane of System Preferences on that machine; see Task #74 for more information. You'll also need to know the IP address for the locked Mac. Use safe networking practices when activating the powerful Remote Login features in Tiger.

## Caution!

You should be very careful when you use the `kill` command. Killing the wrong process can have an adverse effect on the operation of your Mac. Always try the Force Quit command first to ensure that the correct process is killed; if that doesn't work, use the procedure in this task. If the application still refuses to quit, restart the frozen Mac.

# SHARE FILES
## with iChat

You can send and receive files with iChat. When chatting with a buddy, you can send a file to that person in one of two ways.

The simplest way to send a file to someone is to drag the file from the Finder and drop it in the text box of the chat window. When you drop the file in the box where you type text, an icon appears in the chat text box representing that file.

You can also send a file to someone in your Buddy or Rendezvous list by using the Buddies menu or a contextual menu.

Sharing files in iChat is great for exchanging photographs, short movie clips, résumés, or even homework with friends, co-workers, or schoolmates. You could send the same files with e-mail, but transferring files with iChat is faster. You do not have to wait for your e-mail to bounce around all over the world until it reaches its destination. iChat sends the file directly to your recipient, who can then use it immediately.

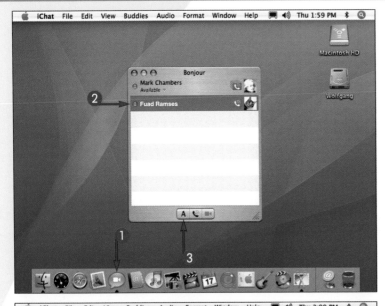

### SEND A FILE USING DRAG AND DROP

❶ Click the iChat icon in the Dock.

❷ Click a buddy in your list to whom you would like to send a file.

❸ Click the Start a Text Chat button.

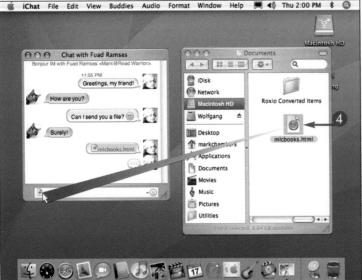

❹ Drag a file from the Finder into the text box at the bottom of your iChat window.

❺ Press Return.

iChat begins transferring the file to your buddy.

DIFFICULTY LEVEL

## SEND A FILE USING THE BUDDIES MENU

1 Click a buddy in the Buddy list to whom you would like to send a file.

2 Click Buddies.

3 Click Send File.

iChat opens a standard file dialog.

4 Select the file to send.

5 Click Send.

iChat begins transferring the file to your buddy.

## TIPS

### Did You Know?

One of the great things about transferring files with iChat is that you are not hampered by the file size limits that you encounter when sending files by e-mail. There does not seem to be a limit — at least not within reason — to what size iChat can transfer. E-mail, on the other hand, tops out at a few megabytes.

### Caution!

Sometimes iChat can be finicky about sending certain types of files. If you run into a circumstance in which iChat will not cooperate, try compressing the file in question first. You can use almost any compression format, such as StuffIt, ZIP, and TAR, as long as the recipient has a decompression application. Try resending the newly compressed file instead of the original.

# Use
# iCHAT KEYBOARD SHORTCUTS

You can speed up your iChat use with a variety of handy keyboard shortcuts. Some shortcuts help you organize your chat sessions, whereas others make features easier to use. Many Mac users find that keyboard shortcuts are especially convenient while chatting or sending instant messages, because you don't have to take your fingers from the keyboard to use your mouse.

One keyboard shortcut enables you to type a multiline message without waiting for the text to wrap. This forces the message text box to grow

by one line immediately, instead of when the text reaches the edge of the box.

For quick entry of the numerous smiley faces available in iChat, you can type the standard keyboard shortcuts. By not resorting to the mouse, you can save yourself time and effort.

You can also use the keyboard to help speed up text formatting changes, like adding the bold or italic attributes, or changing the font itself.

❶ Click the iChat button in the Dock.

iChat launches.

❷ Click a name in the Buddy list.

❸ Click the Start a Text Chat button.

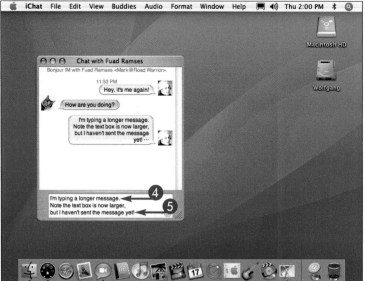

❹ As you type a message in the chat window, press Option-Return.

A line break is inserted in the message, but what you have typed is not sent yet.

❺ Type more text and press Return.

iChat sends the multiline message.

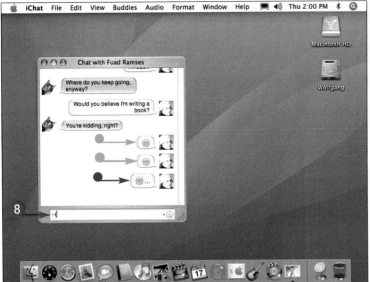

6 Type :-).
○ A smiley face appears.

7 Type ;-).
○ A winking smiley face appears.

8 Type :-(.
● A frowning face appears.

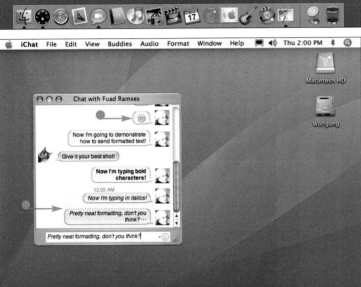

9 Press ⌘-B.

iChat adds the bold attribute to your text.

10 Press ⌘-I.

iChat adds the italic attribute to your text.

## TIPS

### Customize It!

You can customize the background of your chat windows by selecting View→Set Chat Background. iChat displays a standard File Open dialog, enabling you to choose your image. You can also access this feature by Control-clicking in the View section of the chat window itself and choosing View, Set Background Pattern. To return to the regular background, choose View→Clear Background.

### Customize It!

If you like to keep your iChat windows as small as possible, you can toggle the pictures off by clicking View→Show Pictures to remove the check mark. You can also reduce the size of your iChat window by turning off the balloon effect that surrounds the text messages; click View→Show as Balloons to remove the check mark.

# SHARE AN iPOD
## on a network

You can share the files stored on an iPod with other Macs on your network without the hassle of unplugging it and connecting it to the other computers. An iPod, after all, is really just a souped-up disk drive, and Tiger can share the contents of any drive across the network. To begin sharing an iPod with others on the network, activate Personal File Sharing in the Sharing pane of System Preferences. Then plug an iPod into your Mac. Now other users on the network can access your drive.

When you share an iPod, other users will see the data stored on the iPod's hard drive. They will not, however, see the music that you have uploaded to the iPod with iTunes. The music files are hidden from view. However, other users can access the contents of any folders you have created on your iPod, as well as the contents of the Notes, Calendars, and Contacts folders that are found on every iPod.

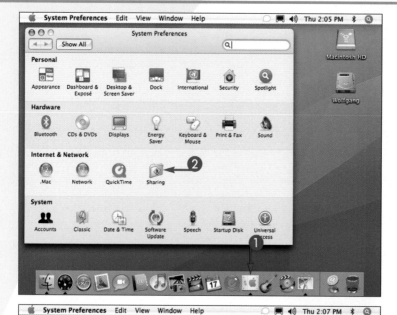

① Click the System Preferences icon in the Dock.

The System Preferences dialog opens.

② Click Sharing.

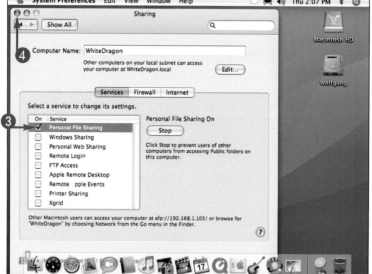

The Sharing pane of System Preferences appears.

③ Click Personal File Sharing (☐ changes to ☑).

File sharing is activated.

④ Click the Close button to quit System Preferences.

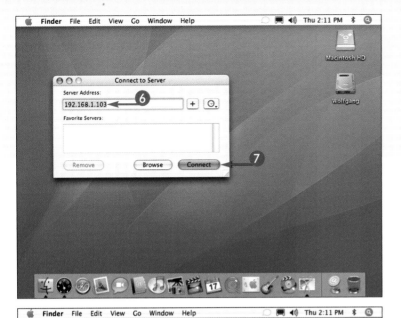

⑤ Go to a different Macintosh on the same local network and press ⌘-K.

⑥ Type the IP address of the computer connected to the iPod.

⑦ Click Connect.

**Note:** *If prompted for your name and password, type them and click Connect.*

⑧ Click the iPod in the volume list.

⑨ Click OK.

● The remote iPod icon appears on your desktop.

## TIPS

### Did You Know?
Depending on how the network settings on the Mac connected to the iPod are configured, you may be required to log in as a registered user before you can use to the shared drives on that machine. This means you will have to create an account on the Mac connected to the iPod, just like you did in Tasks #74 and #77.

### Apply It!
Many iPod owners have no idea that they can use their iPods to store data as well as music. When you have connected your iPod to your Mac and the iPod icon appears on your desktop, double-click it to open it like any other external drive. Create a new folder on your iPod, and copy files and folders to it as you normally would.

Chapter 8: Making the Most of Your Network Connection **177**

# Using Tiger's Advanced Features

In this chapter, the focus turns to features and applications in Tiger that you may not have encountered yet — more advanced tips and tricks that apply to networking, automation, Internet security, and communications. You may not need to use utility applications like Network Utility or System Profiler every day, or even every week, but Apple includes them in Tiger anyway, and you will find them very valuable when you need technical information on your network connection, hardware, or software.

Other tips and tricks covered in this chapter are real timesavers — for example, sending a fax directly from within the document, automatically running a specific application when you load an audio CD, or using services to generate a summary paragraph for a long report.

Finally, you will find a number of advanced tips in this section that are Internet-related — for example, downloading files with FTP, setting up your Internet firewall, or handling your e-mail using threads.

# Top 100

# PROTECT YOUR COMPUTER
## with a firewall

You can protect your computer from hackers by using a firewall. Although the simplest and most sure method of avoiding hacker trouble is to simply disconnect your Mac from your cable modem, DSL modem, or dial-up modem, this is not a good option if you are downloading or using Tiger's built-in Apache Web server. For this reason, most Tiger users choose a firewall.

A firewall can be either a software-based solution or a separate piece of hardware — always more expensive and harder to configure, especially for someone who is simply running a small home network or even connecting just one Macintosh to the Internet.

Luckily, Mac OS X Tiger has a powerful built-in firewall that you can use to protect your computer from outside hackers and unauthorized Internet access. As its name implies, a *firewall* erects a *wall* on your network between you and the outside world. You can get past this wall going out to use the Internet yourself, but computers on the other side of the firewall are blocked from accessing your machine through the Internet.

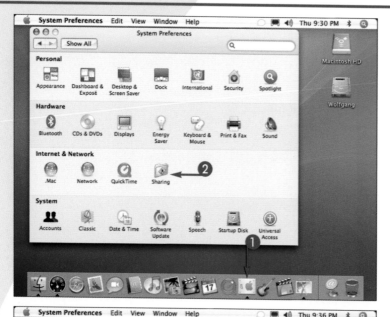

**1** Click System Preferences in the Dock.

**2** Click Sharing.

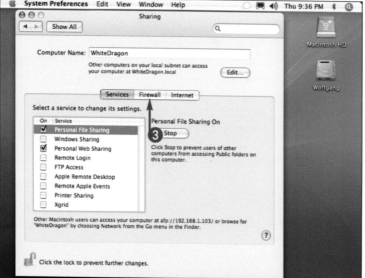

The Sharing pane of System Preferences appears.

**3** Click Firewall.

180

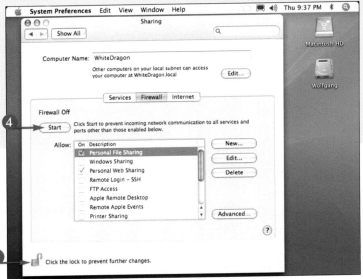

**4** Click Start.

The firewall is activated.

**5** Click the Lock icon to make sure your firewall is not turned off by mistake.

# 81

**DIFFICULTY LEVEL**

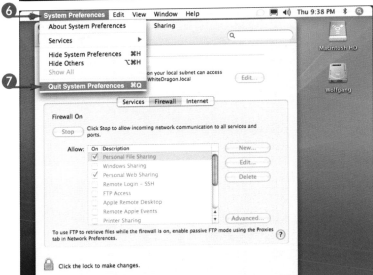

**6** Click System Preferences.

**7** Click Quit System Preferences.

**TIPS**

### Caution!
Follow good security practices when using a firewall. If you are not using a *port,* a kind of doorway that either blocks traffic or allows it through, there is no need to open it. Deactivate any ports that you are not using. Closing a port on the firewall is not like locking a doorway: It is like completely removing the door altogether.

### Customize It!
To allow access for certain types of Internet communications, use the Allow check boxes to fine-tune your firewall. To share a Web page, click Personal Web Sharing (☐ changes to ☑) to permit outsiders to use its port. The firewall is activated with the Personal Web sharing port open. Users outside of your local network can now view your Web pages.

# TRANSFER FILES
## with FTP

The next time that you decide to download a file from an FTP link in Safari, do not be alarmed if you cannot find the downloaded file! Behind the scenes, the Finder is mounting a drive on your Mac. You can then retrieve the file from that mounted drive.

The Finder works well for downloading files from your own FTP servers. The downside is that it is a one-way-only process. You cannot upload files to an FTP server in the Finder. To upload to an FTP server,

you could use the old method and use the command line. Alternatively, you could opt for a slick GUI-based FTP client. There are many available on the Internet, including some good free ones.

Keep in mind that Tiger comes with an FTP server built-in; you can launch it by using the Sharing pane of System Preferences. After the FTP server is launched, users can log in and share files with you.

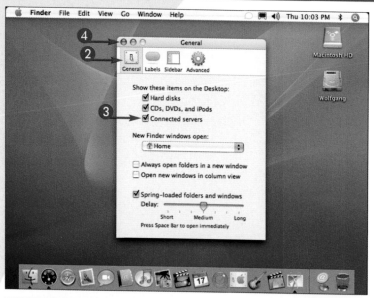

① Press ⌘-, (comma).

② Click General.

③ Click Connected servers (☐ changes to ☑ ).

  Connected servers, including FTP servers, appear on the desktop.

④ Click the Close button to close the Finder Preferences window.

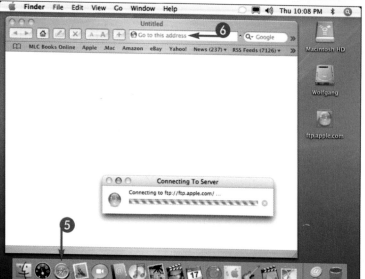

⑤ Click the Safari icon in the Dock.

⑥ Type the address of an FTP server.

⑦ Press Return to mount that FTP server in the Finder.

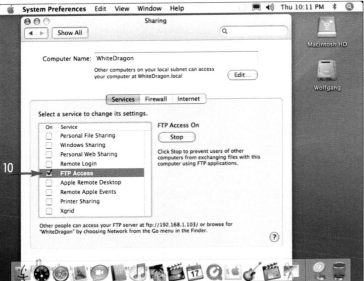

**8** Click the System Preferences icon in the Dock.

**9** Click Sharing.

The Sharing pane of System Preferences appears.

**10** Click FTP Access ( ☐ changes to ☑ ).

The FTP server is activated.

## Customize It!

When you activate your FTP server, users that connect to your Macintosh will have access to the files located in the ~/Library/Public folder. To manage the content that you offer to your FTP users, add and remove files within this folder. Note that you can also create subfolders within the ~/Public folder, enabling you to organize your content for easy perusal.

## Did You Know?

FTP is over 30 years old! Included as one of the technologies in ARPANet, a military precursor to the Internet, FTP has been serving millions of files for years. FTP is well tested, debugged, and competent. UNIX, upon which Mac OS X Tiger sits, has been around for years as well, resulting in its reputation for reliable multiuser performance.

# FAX FILES
## from any application

You can send a fax to other computers or to any stand-alone fax machine using Tiger's built-in send fax feature. If you have connected your Mac's internal modem to your telephone line, your Macintosh is already your personal fax machine; it is one of those neat computer tricks that actually does not require Internet access! When the first version of Mac OS X debuted, faxing was not supported as a feature; instead, you had to rely on expensive and complex third-party software to send faxes.

Today, Tiger includes both built-in fax send and receive capabilities. You can easily and quickly fax documents directly from any application, just as if you were printing the document on a local or network printer. In fact, to fax a document you will use the Fax dialog, which is available from the PDF menu on the standard Print dialog.

Tiger adds the convenience of Address Book access to your built-in fax support, so that you can easily choose any contact with a fax number as the recipient of your outgoing fax.

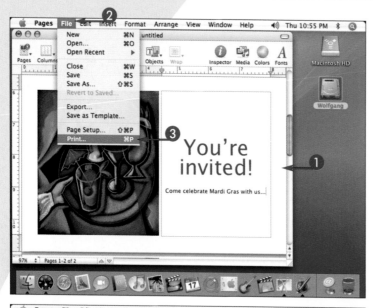

① Open a document in your favorite word processor, graphics application, or Web browser.

② Click File.

③ Click Print.

Alternatively, you can press ⌘-P.

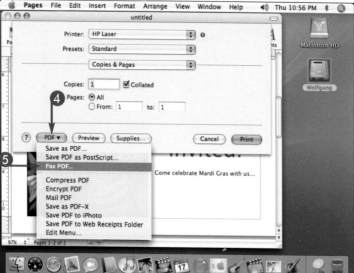

The standard Print dialog appears.

④ Click PDF.

⑤ Click Fax PDF.

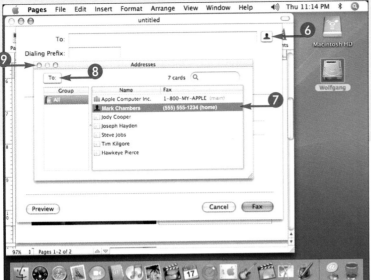

6. Click the Address Book icon.
7. Click the contact who will receive your fax.
8. Click the To: button.
9. Click the Close button on the Address Book dialog.

## #83

**DIFFICULTY LEVEL**

10. Click Use Cover Page (☐ changes to ☑).
11. Type a subject.
12. Type a message.
13. Click Fax.

The modem dials and the fax is sent.

## TIPS

### Customize It!

To check the appearance of your fax before you send it, click the Preview button. Tiger opens the Preview application and displays each page of your fax, just as it will appear when sent, including your cover page if you decide to add one. If the fax document passes inspection, click the Fax button inside the Preview window to send the document.

### Customize It!

If your Mac's modem must use your company's phone system to dial out, you may need a dialing prefix; this is typically the case when a digit needs to be pressed to access an outside line. Click in the Dialing Prefix box and type the prefix, and Tiger will automatically add the prefix to the beginning of the recipient's fax number.

# Display hardware and software information with the
# SYSTEM PROFILER

You can display all sorts of technical information about your Mac's hardware and software by using Tiger's System Profiler. Rather than disassemble your Macintosh or get dirty under your desk, use System Profiler to display what type of memory modules your computer uses, the speed of your Mac's processor, and the media your internal DVD recorder can use.

System Profiler is not limited to just your hardware specifications, however; this versatile application can also display information on your software, including Tiger itself and all of your applications and fonts. You can also reveal a treasure trove of network information, including all the settings used by your current Ethernet and Bluetooth configurations.

You may need to display these technical details if you have to contact Apple's technical support or if you are trying to determine whether an application will run on your system. Of course, if you simply want bragging rights at your next Mac User Groups meeting, System Profiler can provide the specifications you need to trounce the rest of the computer crowd!

① Click .

② Click About This Mac.

The About This Mac dialog appears.

③ Click More Info.

Tiger launches the System Profiler.

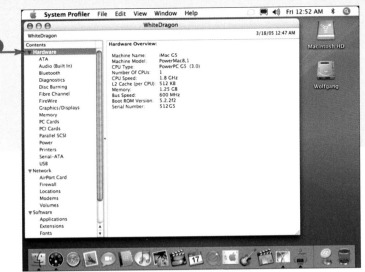

④ Click the Hardware heading in the Contents list.

Tiger displays the hardware overview.

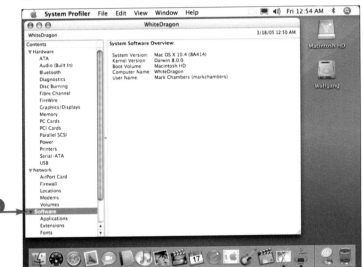

⑤ Click the Software heading in the Contents list.

Tiger displays the software overview.

⑥ Press ⌘-Q to exit System Profiler.

## Did You Know?

You can also use the System Profiler to display all the network connections and network settings currently operating on your Mac, including the IP address, DNS servers, and individual Ethernet address being used by this particular computer. Because you can print any information within System Profiler by pressing ⌘-P, you can create an instant network cheat sheet!

## Did You Know?

To display a brief summary of your hardware or software, just click the Hardware, Network, or Software headings within Tiger's System Profiler. However, you can burrow deeper to display more information about individual hardware, network connections, and software components by clicking the disclosure triangle next to the three headings in the Contents list, which reveals the subheadings.

# Use Mac OS X
# SERVICES

You can use the commands found on Tiger's Services menu to help streamline many common tasks to one or two mouse clicks, without requiring you to launch the associated application. You can easily send a file to a Bluetooth network device, open TextEdit with selected text, create a new sticky note with the contents of a file, or create a Mail message with selected text. You can even have your Mac speak the selected text in a document to help you proofread it!

When you click a Services menu item, Tiger automatically launches the appropriate application

and copies, loads, or otherwise manipulates the original data and switches to the application so you can complete your task.

Note that the services available for a specific file depend on the file's content and format. Some services are also available only when you have already selected a section of text or an image within a document or Web page, and others are only available when a specific application has been installed.

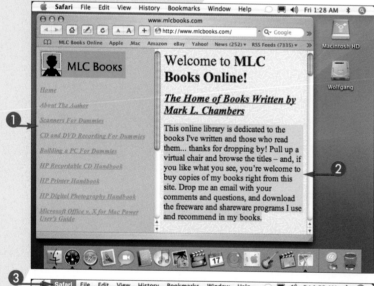

① Open a document in your favorite application.

② Select content from the document, like text or an image.

Some services also work on selected files or folders in the Finder window.

③ Click the application's named menu, such as Safari.

④ Position your mouse cursor over Services.

**5** Click the service that you want.

Tiger launches the required application and prepares the selection according to the type of service.

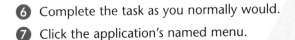

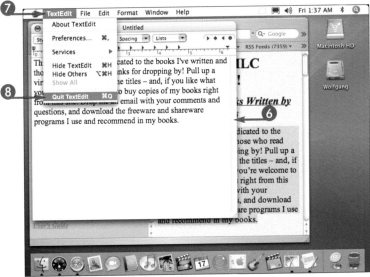

## 85

**6** Complete the task as you normally would.

**7** Click the application's named menu.

**8** Click Quit to exit the application called by the service.

---

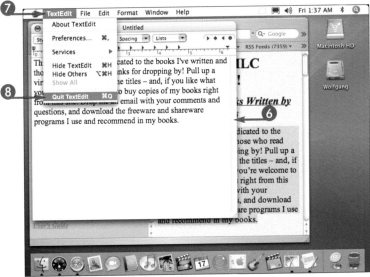

### Did You Know?

Although most services are standard functions that work with Tiger's built-in applications like the Speech service, which speaks the text you have selected within TextEdit and Word. Some third-party applications install their own commands in the Services menu. For example, BBEdit can create a new text file with just the selected text from within Safari.

### Did You Know?

Summarize is a Tiger service that comes in very handy while you are editing a text file in TextEdit, or when you are reading a long block of text in Safari. Select a block of text and choose Summarize from the Services menu. Tiger opens the Summary window and displays what it considers to be the high points of the text with surprising accuracy.

# Work automatically with
# CD AND DVD DISCS

You can save yourself a few keystrokes or mouse clicks every time that you load a CD or DVD into your Macintosh. You can simply set Tiger to automatically launch your favorite application, depending on the type of disc you have loaded. You can also set Tiger to automatically run a script when a specific type of disc is loaded.

The default applications are good choices — iTunes for audio CDs, iPhoto for picture CDs, and DVD Player for DVD movies — but you may specify other

applications that you prefer instead. You can also choose the applications that will launch automatically if you insert a blank recordable CD or a blank recordable DVD. For example, you may want to run iTunes for a blank CD and launch Roxio Toast for a blank DVD disc.

If you prefer that Tiger do nothing when a particular type of disc is loaded, you can choose the Ignore option, and Tiger will pay no heed when you load your audio CD or DVD movie.

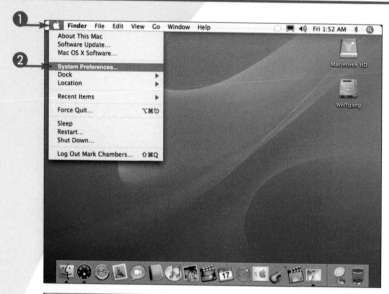

① Click .

② Click System Preferences.

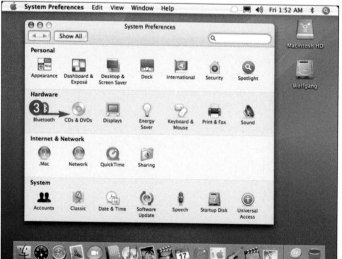

The System Preferences window appears.

③ Click CDs & DVDs.

The CDs & DVDs pane appears.

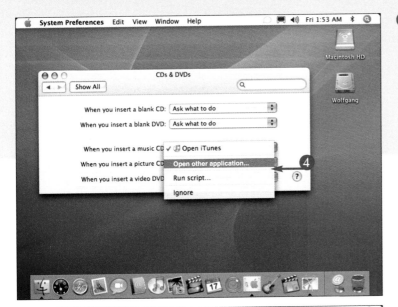

④ Click each up-down arrow and select the action for that type of disc.

Click Open other application to select an alternative application.

Click Run script to specify an AppleScript to be launched automatically.

Click Ignore to disable any automatic action.

# 86

DIFFICULTY LEVEL

⑤ Click the System Preferences Close button to quit and save your changes.

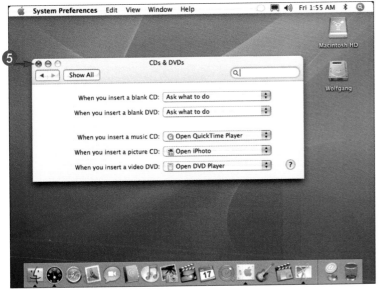

## TIPS

### Did You Know?
If you load a blank recordable CD or DVD and you have left the corresponding drop-down list box set to the default — Ask what to do — Tiger automatically prompts you for permission to format the disc. After formatting is complete, you can drag files and folders to the disc icon on the desktop and burn it whenever you like.

### Did You Know?
The Open Disk Utility option for blank CDs and DVDs makes it easy for you to burn disc images that you have created or downloaded from another source. This also provides Tiger with a basic backup function because Disk Utility provides a restore from disc image feature. The Disk Utility application automatically takes care of formatting for you.

# RUN
## multiple versions of
# MAC OS X

You can switch between operating systems using the Startup Disk pane within System Preferences. Depending on the model of Macintosh you are using, Tiger may be able to boot directly into Mac OS 9. Or, if you have more than one hard drive or a network connection, you may have bootable installations of different versions of Mac OS X that you can access from different locations. For example, if you keep the current version of Mac OS X on one drive and the latest beta of the new version on my external FireWire drive.

Network administrators often keep a pristine version of Mac OS X available in a restricted area on the server, so that a Mac experiencing troubles can be rebooted successfully for troubleshooting.

Many hardware and disk utility applications also ship on bootable CDs and DVDs. You can use the Startup Disk pane to restart your Mac using a bootable disc, which often allows you to diagnose and repair problems that you normally could not address with your internal hard drive as the startup disk.

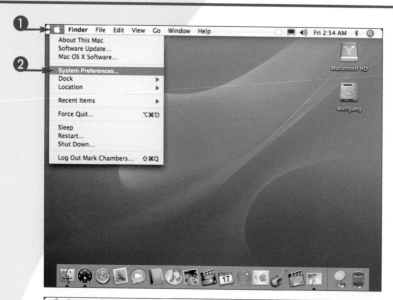

1 Click .

2 Click System Preferences.

The System Preferences window appears.

3 Click Startup Disk.

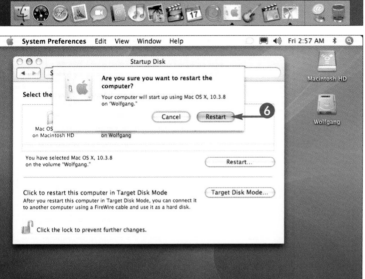

The Startup Disk settings appear.

④ Click the desired bootable operating system to select it.

⑤ Click Restart.

**DIFFICULTY LEVEL**

Tiger displays a confirmation dialog.

⑥ Click Restart.

Your Mac restarts in the chosen operating system.

### Caution!

It is important to connect and power on any networked or external drives before you open the Startup Disk pane of System Preferences; otherwise, the operating systems installed on those drives will not be displayed in the list. Bootable CDs or DVDs should be loaded and they should appear on your desktop before you open the Startup Disk pane.

### Caution!

If you have installed a bootable partition on your iPod, it is possible to boot your Macintosh from your favorite digital audio player; however, it is not recommended because the iPod's miniature hard drive is not rated to stand the same punishment as a full-size hard drive. Whenever possible, use an external drive as a startup disk and leave your iPod for your music.

# USE BONJOUR TO SURF
## local Web and intranet sites

You can locate Mac Web sites running on your local network and view them with Safari. These internal Web sites, called *intranets*, are often set up to provide company or school news and files of interest to employees and students. An intranet Web site is not accessible by others on the Internet.

You do not need to save a bookmark for those Web sites because Safari can find them on the network for you automatically, with no configuration on your part.

You do not even need to know the Web address of the servers on your network!

Safari accomplishes this nifty trick through the magic of Bonjour. *Bonjour* is the name of the technology that Apple uses to automatically find services on a local network. With Bonjour, there is no need for IP addresses or domain names. Tiger just finds them, even if they have just been added to your network, so you can simply choose and connect.

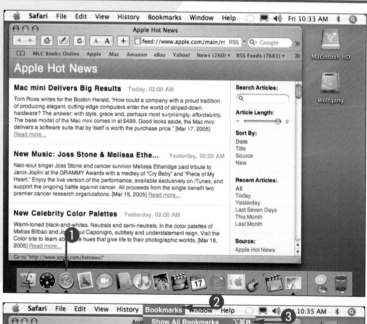

**①** Click the Safari icon in the Dock.

The Safari window appears.

**②** Click Bookmarks.

**③** Click Show All Bookmarks.

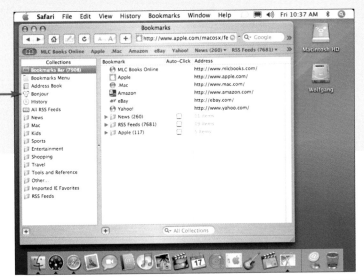

④ In the Collections pane, click Bonjour.

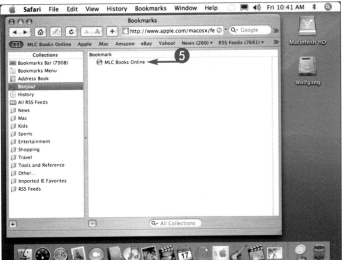

Safari lists the Web sites that it finds on the network.

⑤ Double-click a bookmark to view that Web site.

The Web site appears in the Safari window.

## TIPS

### Did You Know?

Just because you are running one Web server does not mean that only one Web site will appear in Bonjour. The default installation of the Apache Web server in Tiger creates a Web site for each user on a machine as well as one for the root of the machine. This means that you may see as many as six Web sites listed in Safari if the Web server has five different users.

### Did You Know?

Bonjour technology makes it very easy to set up an office-wide Intranet (even if your office network restricts access to the outside world through the Internet). By running Tiger's built-in Apache Web server on one Macintosh in your office, others can easily connect through Bonjour to download files or view the latest in office news on your informal blog.

# TRACKING
## Internet information with Network Utility

You can use Tiger's Network Utility to track down information about a particular server, computer, or individual on the Internet. These settings come in handy if you are having trouble sending mail to a specific mail server; your ISP's technical support representative might ask for that server's mail exchange data or other information.

Unfortunately, this Internet information has to be tracked down manually because a server or Web site does not volunteer details about itself unless you know how to ask. You can poll a server on the

Internet or check connectivity by opening a Terminal window and typing commands, but Tiger saves you the trouble!

Most Tiger users have probably never even launched Network Utility, but it can supply quite a bit of different Internet- and Ethernet-related information. In fact, Network Utility has centralized several separate Internet diagnostic tools into one application, so you do not have to learn a book's worth of arcane UNIX commands to discover what you need to know about other Internet sites.

① Click the Finder icon in the Dock.

A new Finder window opens.

② Click Utilities in the Finder window sidebar.

③ Double-click Network Utility.

The Network Utility window appears.

④ Click the Lookup button.

The Lookup pane appears.

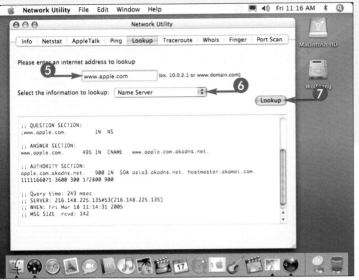

5 Type the Internet address you want to view.

6 Choose the type of information you want to display.

7 Click Lookup.

The Web site information appears in the scrolling window.

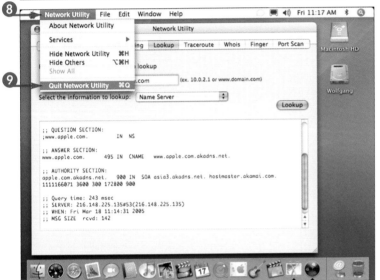

8 Click Network Utility.

9 Click Quit Network Utility to close the Network Utility window.

## TIPS

### Did You Know?

If you have been using the Internet for some time, you will likely recognize some of the other tabs and controls in the Network Utility window: Ping enables you to test whether your computer can connect with the server at another IP address, and Traceroute displays the route taken when you send data to another computer on the Internet.

### Did You Know?

Although Tiger primarily relies on Ethernet for networking, many schools and small offices still use the older AppleTalk standard. If older Macintosh computers on your network are still using an AppleTalk network connection to your computer, click the AppleTalk button to display the status of that connection, including performance statistics, network error counts, and AppleTalk zones that you can access.

# MANAGE
## threaded
# E-MAIL

You can use the threaded e-mail feature in the Mail application to organize your e-mail discussions. When a friend sends you an e-mail and you click Reply to answer in Mail, you are creating a *thread.* Should your friend decide to also reply, that message also becomes part of the thread. In some mail applications, when you want to review each of the messages in a thread, you have to scroll through all of your messages looking for similar subject lines.

Tiger's Mail application helps you keep track of e-mail threads. Mail can display e-mail in a convenient hierarchical folder arrangement, much like List view in the Finder. That way, you can backtrack through the thread and reread the previous messages that pertain to any new ones that arrive by simply expanding the thread's enclosing folder. This takes a lot of the guesswork and scrolling out of replying to e-mails, lending a more organized feel to a busy Inbox.

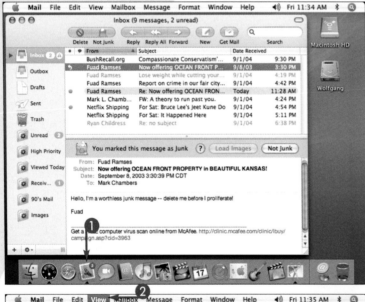

**①** Click the Mail icon in the Dock.

The Mail window appears.

**②** Click View.

**③** Click Organize by Thread.

Threaded e-mail messages are highlighted in blue, with triangles you can click to expand each thread.

4 Click View.

5 Click Expand All Threads.

Threaded e-mail messages expand to reveal all messages in each thread.

6 Click View.

7 Click Collapse All Threads.

Threaded e-mail messages collapse to collapse each thread.

**TIPS**

### Did You Know?

You can change the highlight color used to display threaded messages. Press ⌘-, (comma) to open the Mail Preferences window, and click the Viewing pane. Click the Highlight related messages using color well and choose a new highlight color from the color wheel that appears. After you have picked the right shade of purple, click the Close button on the color wheel.

### Did You Know?

You may be wondering what happens to an e-mail thread if a recipient changes the subject line, which happens often in a longer discussion that covers several topics. Fortunately, Mail actually keeps track of threaded messages using a number of e-mail message headers that are normally hidden from sight, so message subjects can change without disrupting the thread.

# Chapter 10

# Putting Tiger's Applications to Work

Although many folks consider the iLife suite of applications to be the star of the Macintosh show, Tiger has dozens of other applications built in that can prove just as valuable to you. These applications can store your personal information, help you manage your time, improve your productivity and enable your Macintosh to communicate with external devices.

With iCal, you can not only organize and plan for upcoming events — you can even share your calendar with others by publishing it as a shared resource. Likewise, your contact information that is stored in Address Book is easily distributed to others within your office or your family.

Automator is a new feature introduced in Tiger; you can use this great application to build automated scripts that can launch at specific times of the day, or handle boring and repetitive tasks for you with a minimum of fuss. Oh, and you do not have to be a computer programmer to use Automator, either.

The Printer Setup Utility is an important part of Tiger for anyone who prints from within a Mac OS X application. You will use Printer Setup Utility to manage your print jobs.

# Top 100

# Take
# SCREENSHOTS WITH GRAB

You can take snapshots of your Mac's display and save them to your hard drive in TIFF format. With the Grab utility included in Tiger, you can capture the contents of an application window as an image file — from there, you can edit the screen capture in iPhoto or Photoshop CS. You can use the edited image like clip art, importing your screen shot into a word-processing document or spreadsheet document as a picture.

Grab is perfect for capturing screens from applications that do not normally offer screen snapshot capabilities, like many games, 3-D modeling applications, and screen savers. You can also use Grab to capture images from applications that do not provide printer support, and print the contents of the screen using Grab instead.

Need another image format besides TIFF, perhaps for your Web site? You can use Preview to export the TIFF images you capture into a dozen other image formats, including JPEG, BMP, PDF and PNG.

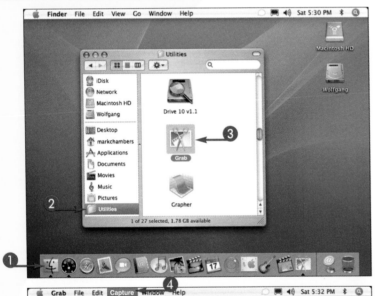

① Click the Finder icon in the Dock.

A new Finder window opens.

② Click the Utilities folder in the Finder window sidebar.

③ Double-click Grab.

The Grab menu appears. The application does not display a window when you launch it.

④ Click Capture.

⑤ Click Screen.

The Screen Grab dialog appears.

⑥ Click outside the Screen Grab dialog.

Grab creates the image and opens it in a new window.

⑦ Press ⌘-S.

The Save dialog appears.

⑧ Type a name for the screenshot and click Save.

⑨ Click Save.

The screenshot is saved.

## TIPS

### Did You Know?

You can also capture just the active window or a selected area, which reduces the image size to a minimum. Choose Window from the Capture menu to include just the active window, or click Selection to specify the area by dragging. The Timed Screen command starts a ten-second timer when you click Start Timer, enabling you to arrange windows or launch an application beforehand.

### Customize It!

Do you need to add a mouse pointer to your screen capture? Click Grab→ Preferences to display the pointer styles that you can add. The selected pointer will appear where your real pointer is located. By default, Grab does not include a pointer — you can switch back to a pointer-free screen shot by displaying the Preferences dialog again and clicking the empty square.

# Add a
# NEW EVENT
## in iCal

You can maintain multiple calendars and manage your time using Tiger's *iCal* application, which you can use to track appointments and manage To Do items — complete with alarms and repeating schedules. In fact, if you subscribe to Apple's .Mac service, you can share your iCal calendars online with others and set up appointments based on the calendars that others share online. Within iCal, you can prioritize your events and To Do items to help you stay organized and, if necessary, create multiple calendars for home and office.

When iCal is combined with iSync, you will see that your events, appointments, and To Do items can be shared among all of your portable devices — which includes many mobile phones and PDAs, as well as your iPod and laptop. You can also save your iCal data to a disk file; exporting is useful for backups and trading calendars directly among friends and coworkers. If you are a .Mac subscriber, you can use iSync to share your iCal data among multiple Macs across the Internet.

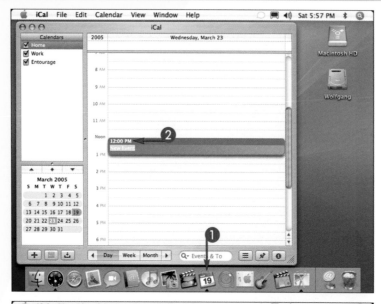

**①** Click the iCal icon in the Dock.

The iCal window appears.

**②** Double-click the time slot for the new event.

iCal displays a new event pop-up for that time slot.

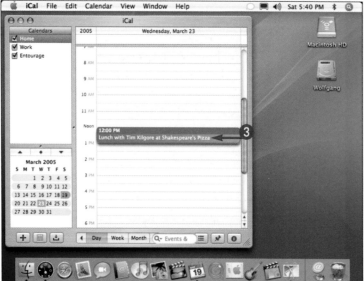

**③** Type a descriptive name for the event and press Return.

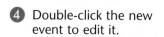

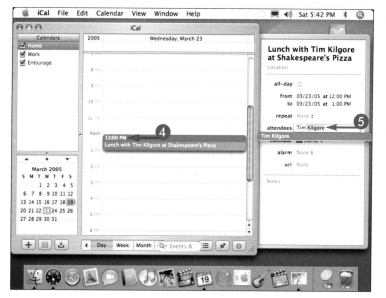

4 Double-click the new event to edit it.

iCal opens the Editing drawer.

5 Click in the fields and enter information about the event.

**DIFFICULTY LEVEL**

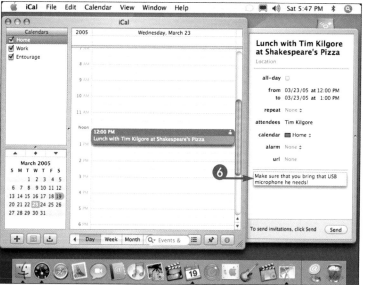

iCal opens an editing box or displays a pop-up menu, depending on the field that you are editing.

6 Click the word *Notes* in the box to type a text note for this event.

7 Press ⌘-Q to quit iCal and save your new event.

**TIPS**

### Did You Know?

It is always a good idea to keep a separate backup of your iCal data; in fact, I keep three backup copies, each a month apart, enabling me to access past appointments and deleted events. To export your iCal data to a disk file, click File→Export and type a name in the Save As box; then click Export.

### Did You Know?

If you are currently using Microsoft's Entourage, you can effortlessly import that data into iCal without retyping a single character. Just click File→Import and then choose Import Entourage data from the Import dialog. iCal will open Entourage and take care of the rest. Note that iCal can also import standard vCal data files from other applications.

# Publish a shared
# iCAL CALENDAR

You can publish your iCal calendar information to others using your iDisk if you subscribe to Apple's .Mac service. Anyone can view your calendar with a Web browser, and other .Mac members can use iCal to subscribe to your shared calendar.

You can change the name of a calendar when it is published, and you can specify what information is contained in the calendars you publish. If your To Do items are no one else's business, you can choose to omit them from the published calendar!

If you are not a .Mac subscriber and you do not have an iDisk, you are not out of luck — you can also publish an iCal calendar on a WebDAV-enabled Web server. Contact your Web site host or Internet service provider to determine if your Web server supports WebDAV functionality. Shared calendars on WebDAV servers can only be accessed with iCal; a Web browser will not work in this mode, so only Mac users can access a WebDAV calendar.

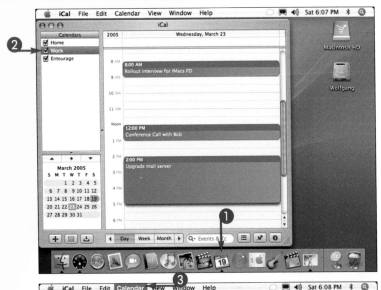

① Click the iCal icon in the Dock.

The iCal window appears.

② Click the calendar you want to publish in the Calendars list.

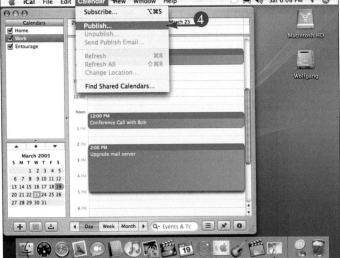

③ Click Calendar.

④ Click Publish.

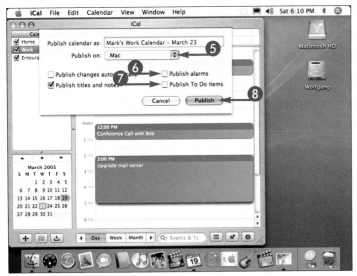

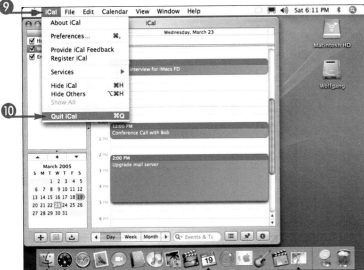

The Publish sheet appears.

**5** Click Publish on to specify where the calendar should be published.

**6** Click Publish alarms to publish event alarms in the calendar.

**7** Click Publish To Do Items to publish your To Do items in the calendar.

**8** Click Publish.

**9** Click iCal.

**10** Click Quit iCal to exit the application.

## TIPS

### Did You Know?

When you publish your iCal calendar, the data it contains remains read-only, meaning that those who subscribe to it can read the calendar data, but cannot modify that data in any way, which makes good sense for the security-conscious. However, iCal can automatically update any changes that *you* make to your published calendar — click the Publish changes automatically checkbox to enable it.

### Did You Know?

If you publish a calendar on a WebDAV server, you will need to enter three values (which can be supplied by your network administrator or Internet service provider): the URL, or Web address, of the server, your login ID, and your password. If you publish using your .Mac account, your .Mac login and password are used automatically; you do not have to enter them separately.

# CREATE AN APPLICATION
## with Automator

You can use *Automator* to create powerful, self-contained applications that are based on AppleScript. Automator is a new feature in Tiger; it is an easy-to-use script-creation tool that makes it possible for anyone to write script applications. With scripting on your side, you can forget tiresome and repetitive tasks that you once had to perform manually.

An Automator application can automatically launch most of the applications provided with Tiger to process data and documents; you can use iPhoto to

work with images, or iTunes to handle audio tasks. Automator can even call on Internet applications like Mail and Safari!

Your Automator applications can be launched manually from any point that you would launch a typical application — from a Finder window, or from the Recent Applications menu. They can also be launched automatically as Login items, so you can create Automator applications that handle specific chores whenever you login.

① Press ⌘-N.

A new Finder window appears.

② Click the Applications folder in the Finder window sidebar.

③ Double-click Automator.

The Automator window appears.

④ Click the application that you want automated in the Library column.

⑤ Drag the desired action into the Workflow area.

*Note: You can add multiple actions that will run in sequence.*

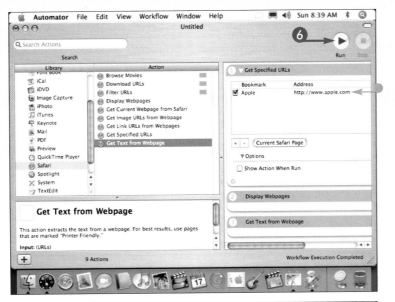

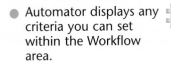

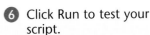

- Automator displays any criteria you can set within the Workflow area.

**6** Click Run to test your script.

**7** Press ⌘-Shift-S.

Automator displays the Save As sheet.

**8** Type a name for the application.

**9** Click File Format and select Application.

**10** Click Save.

**11** Press ⌘-Q to exit Automator.

# TIPS

## Customize It!

You can set your Automator application to display a dialog requesting the criteria it needs to operate — an Automator application that sends an e-mail to an Address Book Group might ask you to specify which Group(s) should receive the message. To set your application for manual input, click the Show Action When Run checkbox to enable it.

## Did You Know?

Apple maintains an Automator Web site that includes tips and suggestions on building your own Automator applications, as well as support information, download areas for the latest software updates, workflow examples, and links to third-party applications that can be used within Automator. To visit the Automator Web site, click Automator and click Display Automator Website.

# FIX COLOR PROBLEMS
## with ColorSync

You can use Tiger's ColorSync feature to ensure that the colors within the images you scan and import into your Mac are accurately reproduced in the images you display and print. Tiger uses files called color profiles to help match corresponding colors between the different devices in your system — for example, your Mac's monitor has a specific color profile, as do your scanner, digital camera and your color printer.

Any graphics professional will tell you that an LCD flat-panel monitor displays colors differently than a

CRT monitor. Tiger automatically sets up the best possible ColorSync color profile for your Mac's monitor, and most external device manufacturers add the correct color profile for its peripherals when you install them. However, it is possible for third-party applications to corrupt your existing profiles (or even install incorrect ColorSync color profiles), so it is a good idea to verify and repair your profiles once every six months or so.

① Click the Finder icon in the Dock.

A new Finder window opens.

② Click the Utilities folder in the Finder window sidebar.

③ Double-click ColorSync Utility.

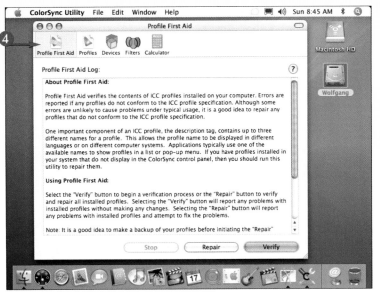

The ColorSync Utility window appears.

④ Click Profile First Aid.

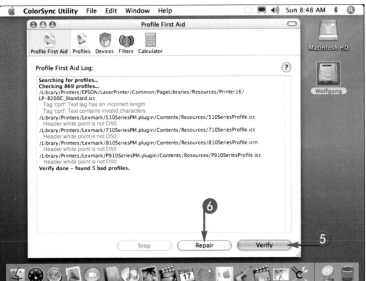

The Logfile window appears.

⑤ Click Verify.

ColorSync Utility displays any errors it discovers in your color profile.

⑥ Click Repair to fix any color profile problems.

⑦ Press ⌘-Q to exit the ColorSync Utility.

## Did You Know?

A typical Mac running Tiger and various image-editing applications may have several hundred color profiles stored on the hard drive — default profiles for both RGB and CMYK, profiles you have created and machine-specific profiles like the iMac or eMac. To display these profiles, click the Profiles button in the ColorSync Utility toolbar; click a specific profile to display its properties.

## Did You Know?

If your color matching suddenly goes haywire after you have installed a third-party application, check to see whether or not a faulty ColorSync profile has replaced or overwritten an existing profile. To check which ColorSync profiles are registered with each hardware device, run the ColorSync Utility and click Devices — the current profile assigned to each device in your system is listed.

# WATCH A DVD MOVIE
## with DVD Player

You can watch DVD movies on your Macintosh using Apple's DVD Player application — that is, of course, if your computer has a drive that can read DVDs. By default, loading a DVD movie into your Mac will automatically run DVD Player — this great application gives you all of the functionality of the standard DVD player you use with a TV set, but it can also remember where you left off if you have to interrupt the movie!

Once the movie has begun, the cool-looking DVD Player "remote control" fades from view, but you can call it back to change a setting or use the controls by moving your mouse — you can also use the keyboard to control the application, like pausing and restarting the movie with the space bar. DVD Player enables you to select from multiple subtitles or audio tracks, and you can slow down the action or advance one frame at a time.

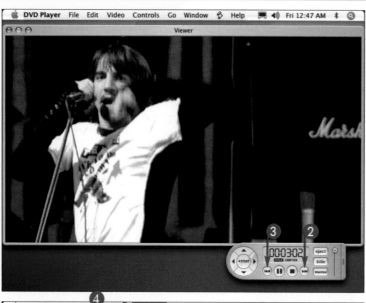

① Load a DVD movie into your Mac.

The DVD Player controller appears and the movie automatically starts to play.

② Click Next Chapter to jump to the next chapter.

③ Click Previous Chapter to jump to the previous chapter.

④ Move your mouse to the top of the screen and click Controls.

⑤ Click Open Control Drawer.

**6** Click Subtitle to The Control Drawer appears on the edge of the controller.

**7** Click Audio to cycle through the different audio track options.

**DIFFICULTY LEVEL**

**8** Click DVD Player to quit DVD Player.

**9** Click Quit DVD Player.

## TIPS

### Did You Know?

If something comes up and you have to postpone the rest of the movie, go ahead and quit DVD Player. The next time you load that DVD, or run DVD Player manually, the application will ask whether you want to restart the movie where you left off, or if you would like to start the film at the beginning.

### Did You Know?

The three buttons under the controller's display enable you to return to the last menu you used (Menu), return to the Title/Top menu (Title), or eject the disc (Eject). You can also access these functions from the DVD Player menu, as well as change settings like the fast forward/reverse speed rate and the size of the DVD Player window.

# CONVERT CURRENCY
## with Calculator

You can use Apple's Calculator application to convert all sorts of measures and currencies from one standard to another. Sure, Calculator is perfectly suited for quick math calculations, but most Mac owners do not realize that Calculator also comes packed with a surprising number of conversion routines. Forget searching through the dictionary or your encyclopedia when you need to convert a weight in U.S. pounds into kilograms, or the amount of liquid in a container from liters to gallons.

My favorite "hidden" feature of Calculator, however, is its ability to convert one form of currency into another — great for those overseas trips you take with your PowerBook or iBook. The list of currencies that Calculator recognizes is truly staggering — 46 different flavors, including such favorites as the Malaysian ringgit and the Polish zloty! Plus, if you have an active Internet connection, Calculator can automatically update its currency exchange rates. Why buy an expensive currency converter when Calculator can do the job for you?

① Click the Finder icon in the Dock.

A new Finder window appears.

② Click the Applications folder in the sidebar.

③ Double-click Calculator.

The Calculator window appears.

④ Enter the amount you want to convert by clicking the calculator buttons.

**DIFFICULTY LEVEL**

⑤ Click Convert.

⑥ Click Currency.

The Conversion sheet appears.

⑦ Click the From arrow and select the currency.

⑧ Click the To arrow and select the currency.

⑨ Click OK.

The converted amount appears in the Calculator.

⑩ Press ⌘-Q to exit Calculator.

**TIPS**

### Did You Know?

What good is a currency converter that does not use the latest exchange rates? If you have an Internet connection, you can update Calculator with the latest rates at any time! Click Convert, and then click Update Currency Exchange Rates; afterward, Calculator displays the rates that were updated. The time and date of the last update is also displayed on the Convert menu.

### Did You Know?

Calculator provides a number of great features that you would not expect from its somewhat mundane appearance! Click View and click Show Paper Tape to display a virtual paper tape; click File to print or save the tape for future reference. Click Speech, and Calculator speaks each button as you click it. Click View and click Advanced to specify Hex, Binary or Unicode display.

# EDIT TEXT FILES
## with TextEdit

You can make a quick change to a text file with TextEdit, Tiger's bare-bones text-editing application. Mac owners commonly think of Microsoft Word or Apple Pages when they think of editing documents; however, these well-known applications are not always the best choice for a fast editing job on a file that includes only plain text. From time to time, you probably need to edit an application configuration file or edit a text file that you have downloaded from the Internet.

Do not be fooled by TextEdit is simple appearance: That is just good design hiding powerful features. In fact, the application includes a number of advanced options, such as support for Rich Text Formatting (RTF) files, spell checking, justified paragraph formatting and document styles.

There are more powerful text-editing applications available from third-party developers, like BBEdit 8 from Bare Bones Software; however, TextEdit is free with Tiger, and many Mac owners find TextEdit easier to use than more sophisticated text editors.

① Press ⌘-N.

  A new Finder window appears.

② Click the Applications folder in the sidebar.

③ Double-click TextEdit.

The TextEdit window appears.

④ Click File.

⑤ Click Open.

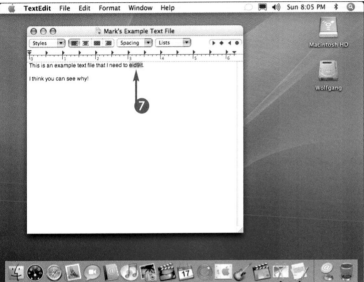

The File Open dialog appears.

⑥ Locate and double-click the text file.

**DIFFICULTY LEVEL**

TextEdit displays the contents of the file.

⑦ Click and drag to select the characters you want to change.

⑧ Type new characters to replace the selection.

⑨ Press ⌘-S to save the updated file.

⑩ Press ⌘-Q to exit TextEdit.

**TIPS**

## Customize It!

By default, TextEdit checks spelling as you type, underlining questionable words in red; however, if you find real-time spell checking distracting, you can customize TextEdit to check your spelling manually. Click TextEdit and click Preferences to display the preferences, and then click the Check Spelling as You Type check box to disable it. To check spelling manually, press ⌘-; (semicolon).

## Did You Know?

TextEdit can speak any text in the file you are editing — a handy feature for those who need to proofread text. Your Mac can speak the entire file, or just a block of selected text that. To speak text, click Edit and click Speech, and then click Start Speaking. To stop speaking, click Edit and click Speech, and then click Stop Speaking.

# CONTROL YOUR PRINT JOBS
## with Printer Setup Utility

You can monitor and control your printer and the print queue using Tiger's Printer Setup Utility. Today's printers offer many features that you can control from your Mac; you can remotely stop a print job, restart a printer queue or print a test page to help diagnose a problem with your printer. Depending on the model of printer, Tiger may even be able to display how much ink, paper or toner remains in your printer!

To consolidate all of these controls into a single application, Apple created the Printer Setup Utility.

Note that you probably will not need the Printer Setup Utility to actually install your printer; today's Macintosh computers use USB or network connections for printing, which greatly reduces the time and trouble involved in adding a printer to your system. Basically, you simply plug any printer supported by Tiger into your Mac's USB port or browse for the printer on the network and load a printer driver (if necessary). You should follow the installation instructions provided by your printer's manufacturer to add a new printer within Mac OS X.

① Click the Finder icon in the Dock.

A new Finder window opens.

② Click the Utilities folder in the Finder window sidebar.

③ Double-click Printer Setup Utility.

● The Printer Setup Utility window appears.

④ Click Printers.

⑤ Click Show Jobs.

● The Print Job window appears.

⑥ Click a print job in the list.

⑦ Click Hold to pause the printing of the job.

**Note:** *Click Resume to restart printing.*

**# 99**

**DIFFICULTY LEVEL**

⑧ Click Delete to delete the selected job.

⑨ Press ⌘-Q to exit the Print Job window.

⑩ Press ⌘-Q again to exit the Printer Setup Utility.

## TIPS

### Did You Know?

You can stop all print jobs in the entire queue — no matter which Mac submitted the job — by clicking Printer in the Printer Setup Utility, and then clicking Stop Jobs. To restart the entire queue at once, click Printer again — notice that Stop Jobs is now Start Jobs on the menu — and click Start Jobs to set your printer in motion again.

### Customize It!

The Print Job window appears automatically in the Dock whenever you click Print to send a document to your printer. There is no need to click the Print Job icon to restore the application unless you need to hold, resume or delete a print job; otherwise, the Print Job Dock icon will disappear as soon as the printer is finished with the job.

# UPDATE CONTACT INFORMATION
## with Address Book

You can set Tiger's Address Book application to automatically notify all of the contacts in a specified Group any time that your personal contact information changes on your Address Book card. Storing and retrieving your contact data with Address Book is easy, but you may need to update your contact data with other computer users when you switch Internet service providers or move to a different address.

Probably the easiest way to alert others to a change in your contact information is to send everyone an e-mail message — a very time-consuming chore if you had to address and send all of those messages manually, especially if your personal information changes often! Instead, you can save yourself all that effort by setting up a Group in Address Book that contains your friends, family and coworkers; Address Book works automatically with Apple's Mail application to notify the contacts in a specified Group whenever you change your personal information.

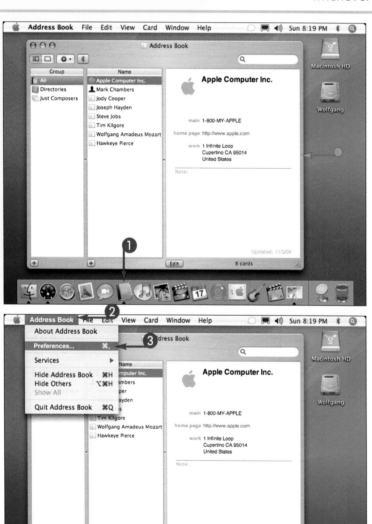

**1** Click the Address Book icon in the Dock.

The Address Book window appears.

**2** Click Address Book.

**3** Click Preferences.

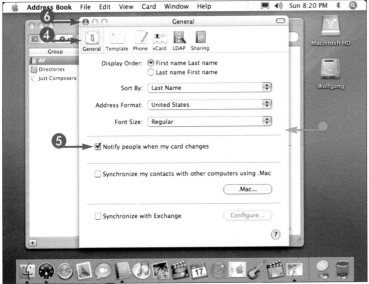

- The Address Book Preferences window appears.

**4** Click General.

**5** Click the Notify people when my card changes checkbox to enable it.

*Note: This checkbox can only be enabled if you have at least one Group set up in Address Book.*

**6** Click the Close button on the Preferences window to save your change.

**DIFFICULTY LEVEL**

**7** Click Address Book.

**8** Click Quit Address Book to exit the application.

**TIPS**

### Did You Know?

If you make a change to your personal Address Book card, a dialog appears asking if you would like to notify a group of people about the change. Click Notify to display the Send Updates dialog, and click the Group(s) that should receive the update information. You can change the default subject and message text — when you are ready, click Send.

### Did You Know?

If you would prefer to take care of things manually, you can easily send a boilerplate e-mail message to update every contact in a specified Group; click File and click Send Updates. Click the Group(s) that should receive your message — you must already have at least one Group defined. Edit the subject and message text, and then click Send to send the update messages.

# Index

# Index

# Index

# Index

**U**

**V**

**W**

**Z**

# Want more simplified tips and tricks?
## Take a look at these
### All designed for visual learners—just like you!

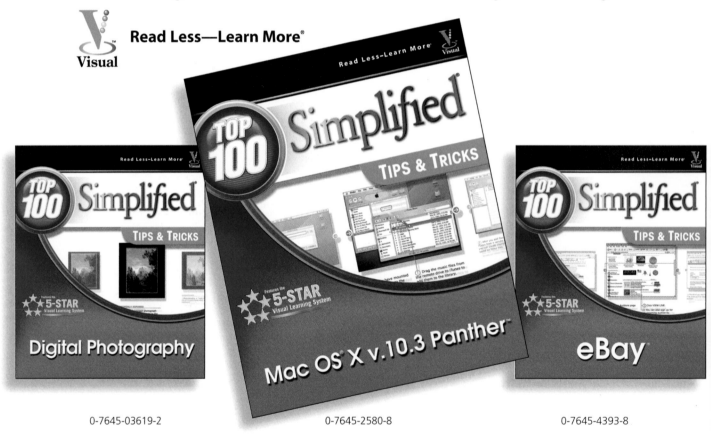

**Read Less—Learn More®**

0-7645-03619-2          0-7645-2580-8          0-7645-4393-8

**For a complete listing of *Top 100 Simplified® Tips & Tricks* titles and other Visual books, go to wiley.com/go/visualtech**

**Visual**
An Imprint of ⊕**WILEY**
Now you know.